INFORMATION

TECHNOLOGY

STANDARDIZATION

INFORMATION TECHNOLOG

Maryann -
For believing That This
would happen - and for
reading The draft to make
sure That it did happen -
in a way That it would be
readable. Thank you -
Carl

CARL F. CARGILL

TANDARDIZATION

THEORY,

PROCESS, AND

ORGANIZATIONS

di**g**i**t**a**l** ™ Digital Press

9 8 7 6 5 4 3 2 1

Order number EY-C167E-DP

Printed in the United States of America.

Design: Outside Designs
Production coordination: Editorial Inc.
Composition: DEKR Corporation
Printing and binding: Alpine Press

Library of Congress Cataloging-in-Publication Data

Cargill, Carl F., 1948–
    Information technology standardization : theory, process, and
    organization / Carl F. Cargill.
        p.   cm.
    Includes index.
    ISBN 1-55558-022-X
        1. Electronic data processing—Standards.   2. Information
    technology—Standards.   I. Title.
    QA76.9.S8C37   1989
    004'.0218—dc19   89-1307
                                                                          CIP

To my parents, who gave me the determination to seek out the truth, and the sense of humor necessary to deal with it when I found it.

CONTENTS

Contents

This book is a long-awaited and long-needed addition to the literature on standards for information technology. The first book on the subject, *The World of EDP Standards,* was published by the Control Data Corporation almost twenty years ago. The National Bureau of Standards (now the National Institute of Standards and Technology) contributed to a second edition, and the third edition was released by Sperry Univac in 1978.

That last edition, or "green book," has been an important briefing tool for me. I have used it many times when talking to people who are unaware of the complexities of the standards world.

However, since 1978, there have been many changes in the standards arena, and the standards process has become more complex. One of the most significant changes is the expanded influence of the users of information technology. Users have become strong supporters of standards that will give them control over the technology and allow them to develop "open systems." This demand for open systems is changing the information technology marketplace. Carl Cargill took on the formidable task of describing today's world of information technology standards. He factually describes the process for developing standards and gives us his opinions about the process and its shortcomings. He brings life to a potentially dull subject, and he does it with style and originality. His book will be read because it is factual and because it is interesting. Newcomers to the standards process will find it a valuable guide to understanding both the formal and the less-than-obvious parts of the process. This understanding is essential to making the process work.

The standards community is enriched by this book. I am grateful to Mr. Cargill for writing it and to Digital Equipment Corporation for supporting his effort.

James H. Burrows
Director
National Computer Systems Laboratory
National Institute of Standards and Technology

PREFACE

This book began as an update of *The World of EDP Standards*, which was published as a guide to the groups involved in information technology (IT) standardization. But I have expanded this original intent to include a philosophy of standards (Part 1), a discussion of practical problems and issues in standards (Part 2), a description and listing of many recognized standard-making bodies (Part 3), and, finally, a discussion of some of the current issues facing the IT standards world (Part 4). The book is not meant to serve as a "how to" manual on standards; rather, it is an attempt to synthesize much that has been written about standards to provide a common base for future standards development, both actually and philosophically. This volume should be regarded as a companion to Dorothy Cerni's *Standards in Process: Foundations and Profiles of ISDN and OSI Studies* (NTIA Report 84-170). The present book owes much to Dorothy's pioneering work in the field, which she continues today.

My decision to exceed the scope of earlier works stemmed in large part from my generally unsuccessful attempts to explain standards to people within my company. I realized rather quickly that, while I understood the rationale for standards on a particular issue, my audience did not. Even worse, I had no means to generalize my experience, since each standards effort was seen as a discrete occurrence: no unifying thread seemed to join these adventures; instead, the entire process was begun afresh with each new effort. At the start of the third such experience, I decided that I needed a theoretical and practical template to steer these efforts. I had assumed that this information was readily available. I was half right. Although many have written on standards, each has embedded her or his perception of standards in an account of a specific standards activity. Finding no single source linking an overview of standards to a global description of the process, I was forced to provide my own.

While this volume can serve as a source book for those wishing to begin a standardization effort, one of its functions is to lay the groundwork for a comprehensive look at standards as they relate to industry, including the roles and expectations of suppliers, users, customers, the government, and society in general.

Each part can be used in isolation, although Parts 1 and 2 are natural companions. My intent in Part 1 was to generalize the concept of standards, so that it would be applicable to all industries worldwide, although I have favored the information technology industry and the United States when there was a conflict.

In Part 2, I have tried to bring together some practical concepts for standards creation, again, as generally as possible. If all of the random precepts in this part were taken to heart, the result would be an unmitigated disaster. The key to standards activity lies in knowing what questions to ask—not in having the answers. If the right questions are asked, the concepts in Part 2 can be applied selectively to create a useful synthesis.

Part 3 examines the major standards organizations responsible for the development of consensus standards in the world. The organizations are presented in a certain order, beginning with the international organizations and moving through the regional bodies, then the national groups. The section closes with a chapter on specialty groups that are part of the consensus standards process but do not use geography as basis for membership. All of the organizations are examined in light of their contributions to information technology standardization, which is the only area examined in any detail; however, many have responsibility for more than IT consensus standards activities, and these larger reponsibilities must be kept in mind. I have included only those organizations that either were kind enough to supply information or about which I knew. Future editions of the book no doubt will list more.

Finally, Part 4 touches on some current issues in standards that are of interest to me and, I hope, to the community at large. It is my fervent hope that succeeding editions of this book will report that some of these issues have been resolved. I hope that the book will help persuade the industry that we are all in this together—and that we should speak a common language. Whether used as a primer, a textbook, or a general reference, this book represents an attempt to begin the discussions that are necessary to the industry as a whole. It should be noted that it is an industry contribution; Control Data Corporation, NBS (now NIST), and Unisys have published earlier editions. The current edition is Digital's contribution to increasing the knowledge of this discipline.

I owe much to many people who helped this book come into being. Gary S. Robinson, my manager at Digital Equipment Corporation, who volunteered me for this task, was a source of both ideas and encouragement during the three years that it has taken me to write this book, helping to firm the concepts from its core. Without him, the book could not have been written. Mary White, my co-worker, listened to my tirades about standards and then told me to get back to work. My senior management at Digital also gave me the freedom to write what I felt was proper, and their interest in "The Book" is highly appreciated. I would like to thank James Burrows at NIST for writing the foreword and for the patience he displayed while I wrote. (I also now understand his smile when he met me and found out that I had agreed to do the rewrite.) Dorothy Cerni, Maureen Harvey, both of Digital, Steve Oksala of Unisys, and James Pearse of Leviton reviewed the original manuscript and commented extensively on it. William Rinehuls of the GSA provided substantial information on the GSA, as did Isabel Valet for AFNOR and Frances Schrotter for JTC 1 and the entire international standards process. Cathie Kachurik and Gwendy Phillips of X3 were invaluable resources and critics, helping to keep me focused and moving. There are numerous other people who provided ideas, criticism, and encouragement. To all, I offer my gratitude and sincere thanks.

I would also like to thank Wendy Reid, who encouraged me when I began to feel that I would never finish, and Helen and Adam, my children, who wondered where I went in the evenings and on weekends when I disappeared to work on the book. Finally, both the readers and I owe a debt of gratitude to my editor, Sarah St. Onge, who took my turgid and pedantic prose and made it readable.

As with any work, there are omissions and mistakes. For these, I take full responsibility and hope to correct them in future editions. I invite your comments, but, most of all, I invite your participation in the standards arena. After all, as Gary would say, "If you don't participate, how can you criticize?"

Carl F. Cargill
Maynard, Massachusetts

L I S T   O F   F I G U R E S

INFORMATION

TECHNOLOGY

STANDARDIZATION

PART I. STANDARDS: THE HISTORICAL AND CONCEPTUAL BASIS

1 . STANDARDS, STANDARDS

EVERYWHERE

> Water, water everywhere,
> Nor any drop to drink.
> *Rime of the Ancient Mariner*
> Samuel T. Coleridge

Over the past years (from 1981 to 1988, especially), there has been an astonishing growth of interest in information technology (IT) standards. As there was a rush to strategic competitive planning in marketing, a rush to quality in manufacturing, and a rush to MBAs in business schools, now there is a rush to standards in IT. People are looking for easy solutions to difficult problems, and they have latched on to what seems like a simple, elegant, easy-to-implement, and all-encompassing answer. Such appealing solutions, unfortunately, are usually wrong.

The IT industry as a whole (and like many other industries) has embraced standards on principle, much as a person embraces a "good" idea: they seem to be the thing to support, but there is no clear explanation of exactly why it is good to support them. Groups are formed to create standards without the faintest idea of how to go about this difficult task; large amounts of money are spent "doing standards" for some end—ostensibly to make money. The industry is in the same predicament as the little child on a roller coaster, asking plaintively "Am I supposed to be having fun?"

The industry publications have recognized the interest, if not the predicament, and have published a spate of articles on standards. The writers describe standards according to their beliefs and experiences;

the results, like the mythical griffin, are composed of known parts that somehow form a wonderful creature full of great potential.

On another level, however, the articles are all much the same. Nearly all focus tightly on one standard or group of common standards, ignoring the purpose of the entire standards process except as it relates to the chosen topic or specific discipline, such as storage technology or transmission engineering. In most other disciplines, there is a tendency toward generalization that usually indicates an understanding of root causes and actions; I have seen very few articles on standards that relate to the basic beliefs implicit in standards.

Certainly, the subject is complex—perhaps there is no market for difficult conceptual articles on standards, and therefore no one has written any. Having read articles on nearly every other conceivable subject in standards, I find this explanation faulty. Some articles dealing with specific standards are so esoteric and abstruse that a piece on the philosophical and practical roots of standards would be pleasant and easy reading by comparison.

Another explanation, of course, could be a lack of interest in the subject as a whole. But this is contradicted by a few articles on standards in which the authors seem to understand the need to create a "unified field theory" for standards that would make their position reasonably secure. Yet, although this existential search is on, it is usually confined to contexts supportive of no more than a single standard or class of standards.

Most likely, however, authors assume the existence of a body of literature that is adequate for the purpose and already has been internalized by the industry. At many standards conventions and standards meetings, everyone refers to the economic motivation for standards or to their impact on innovation or to a specific methodology for obtaining the truth about them. Yet none of these constitutes a central, generalized set of explicitly stated beliefs about standards. True, a set of literature examines the economic justification for standards, and, for that matter, this justification is used increasingly to spur the rush to standards. But the economic model describes one attribute of the standards process and discipline, not the thing itself. Indeed, very few standards decisions are made from a purely rational-economic viewpoint—while it is pleasant to claim that standards are the fruit of quantitative economic roots, it is also highly suspect and more than a little naive. In a similar manner, the technical-mechanistic approach to standards is less than satisfactory, since it reduces standards to something akin to rote memorization. This model sees the *way* to standardize something as the rationale for standardization. It mistakes the means for the end.

The pan-European harmonization, due in 1992, has had a major impact on the standards environment in Europe that, in turn, has impacted the standards environment in the United States and the Pacific Basin. The notion of a single Europe, undivided by separate national standards, appeals to the intellect; it also requires economic rationalization, which economics theory or the technical-mechanistic approach obligingly supplies. A quantifiable base allows things to be calculated with a reasonable degree of certainty: these calculations provide the basis for the next level of growth. Furthermore, IT is based on several sciences and it is comforting to believe that the industry actions are as logically consistent as the product produced. The rush to standards appears to be an extension of the need for order, a response to the lack of certainty that afflicts the IT industry. This response, I believe, is based on flawed reasoning.

The popular press and standards

In each year since 1980, the number of articles on computer standards has doubled. Articles appear in journals that deal with the IT industry in general, with specific subsegments of the industry, and with minor niches of it. They appear in nearly all trade magazines and even in general-circulation newspapers. As noted earlier, the focus usually is on a single standard (Ethernet or the Intelligent Peripheral Interface), on one class of standards (OSI), or on a particular discipline and its relation to standards. Editorials praise a specific effort or fulminate against the imposition of an evilly conceived idea. The industry's grand old people vaunt standards as a way to provide structure to a rapidly changing industry, and the young Turks oppose them, sure that standards represent the last attempt of the old folk and less-brilliant thinkers to stifle creativity. Many advertisers appear to use standards buzz words without understanding why the standards are important or how they are used.

To classify the mongrel issue of the popular press, I have broken down the articles into four categories: articles on a specific standard; articles about standards relating to a specific concept; articles about a specific discipline and the standards that affect it; and articles on the functioning and performance of standards bodies and the standards process. (The term "popular press" refers to the generally available press; it includes most magazines, newspapers, and journals that cover the IT field. It does not include articles published in specialized standards magazines, such as the ANSI *Reporter*.)

In three of these categories, the articles do what they are supposed to do. Articles that deal with a specific standard usually employ predefined and well-understood vocabularies within a set of reasonably clear-cut boundaries to address an audience that understands and is interested in the subject. Articles examining standards that relate to a specific concept are becoming more common, providing their readers with an understanding of the options available to them when considering the implementation of a possible technology. Articles examining standards in terms of their impact on a specific discipline, at a minimum, alert readers to the existence of standards and often provide useful general background to a large audience previously unconcerned with standards.

The articles dealing with standards bodies and the standards process are the least satisfactory. There is a dull sameness to them, as they follow the format of identifying, examining, and commenting on a standards-making body, paying little attention to the concepts that underlie the process or the rationale for participating in it. The articles tend to treat the standards groups as a collective monolithic entity, forgetting that the groups generally are composed of members of the industry—users, producers, developers, academics, and government—who have a need to implement a workaday solution to a problem. The voluntary aspect of the standards committees is all-too-frequently overlooked. Examination of the standards process usually is limited to an overview that acquaints the reader with the methodologies of the process but seldom delves into the multiple rationales that are available for participating on standards committees. This produces a valid description of the process, but one that is relatively sterile and without human, social, or economic context.

In its relatively simplistic approach to standards, the popular press provides updates on the current situation, as well as a limited amount of information on the issues that it believes to be important to its readers. Its function is to inform, not to educate. Unfortunately, and all too often, it misinforms because of its own inability (or disinclination) to comprehend some of the more interesting concepts that are shaping the market.

If the popular press does not even ask the correct questions, let alone provide the answers to these questions, who holds the responsibility for this activity? There are two obvious answers to the question. The first is the academic community, which has provided much of the original research and information used in business and government, as well as much necessary theory for the IT industry in fields outside of standards. The second, and less obvious, answer is the standards organizations themselves.

The academic involvement

In May 1986, a host of distinguished academicians from around the world gathered at the Massachusetts Institute of Technology to look at the problem of the economics of standards. I had the dubious pleasure of attending this colloquium. During several of the more theoretical presentations, various assumptions were used to make economic models perform. Among the assumptions were perfect competition, perfect arrival rate of orders, perfect knowledge of costs and competition, and so on. But standards activities reflect the industries of which they are a part, and these are neither perfect nor predictable; the standards process is buffeted by random, nonquantifiable, and at times irrational behavior and variables. The economists, although associated with high-technology industry, had accepted too much of the popular-press reporting on standards. In the several discussions that followed the formal presentations, it became apparent that this was in fact the best that academia could offer at this time.

The presentations were intended to provide a starting place for an examination of standards as a management tool in the 1990s. Halfway through the day, however, it became clear that there was a lack of agreement on what the term "standards" actually meant. Each lecturer was using the term to suit the particular case under discussion. Yet, without a common terminology, there could be no common understanding of the nature of the situation that was being examined.

Some studies and courses are working to ensure that positive activity at least begins within the academic community. Carnegie-Mellon University, the University of Pittsburgh, and the University of Colorado have encouraged some critical academic interest in the problem of standards and standards formation and theory. While these initial efforts are more the product of individual classroom heroics than of formal programs, they do represent an initial attempt to provide future engineers and computer scientists with some necessary background on the purpose and impact of standards. There is still a long way to go: a recent survey of engineering schools in the United States indicated that only a handful of engineering schools have a course on standards, and, of all engineering courses offered in the United States, only slightly over two hundred mention standards. However, the situation has not gone unnoticed, at least among the professionals in the standards arena, and individual efforts are beginning to correct the situation. It is a start.

Over the past several years, any number of academicians have published books on the competitive advantage, on how to succeed in the computer business, or on how to manage any number of other aspects of business. For an interesting exercise, look up standards in any of these books. Michael Porter's book on competitive advantage, for example, is extremely instructional. (I mention this work because it was exceedingly popular and illustrates my point well.) The term "standard," as it relates to the consensus standards process, does not appear to have been considered worthy of inclusion when the text was written. Within four years, however, the term "industry standard" had become widespread in the literature of the personal computer market, the open system interconnect market, and numerous other places. The idea of industry standards (either *de facto* or *de jure*) had become accepted and been put into use by major companies. I suspect that the concept wasn't spawned overnight but had always been there, lurking and waiting. I tend to believe that the market success of several companies in having their products accepted as "industry standards" was due to careful planning and excellent execution, helped by an understanding of the nature and rationale for standards. Standards have been used and implemented for a long time; this application was unique only because it was done openly, in the press spotlight. The attention, not the activities, was new.

That the IT industry was taken by surprise by the power of standards is in itself a sad statement about the many management and engineering courses taught and the wide number of books published to help managers. If the use of standards was common and understood, why did the phenomenon attract such attention? I believe that academia, which is supposed to be the source of theoretical and advanced leadership to the industry, somehow failed to understand the dynamics of the market and its ability to pursue its own course in response to its perceived and real needs. The question is, why?

The activities of standards groups

Within the United States, over four hundred groups are devoted to "doing standards." The activities range from boilers to broilers and from fabric to fasteners. There are formally recognized and sanctioned organizations and unofficial groups of professionals who have banded together informally to help their industry. The United States is a nation in love with a standard way of doing. Much of the activity centers around informing members of the standards activities within their industry. Each organization may deal with several hundred standards a year, producing them, reviewing them, recommending them for implementation, or obsoleting them. Each group usually follows its own procedures, based on what it feels is a fair and equitable method. Each group maintains mailing lists, organizational memberships, and a series of other organizational and administrative functions. Finally, each group acts to protect and expand its area of influence, sometimes at the expense of other standards groups, at other times in brand-new, nonstandardized territories.

Given this as scenario, the question is not so much why the standards groups have not gotten together for their common good as why they haven't managed to kill one another off yet. In a typical high-technology environment, engineering societies are developing standards, information-processing bodies are writing standards, telecommunications groups are creating standards, manufacturing groups are recommending standards, quality circles are describing standards, and safety groups are mandating practices. The government put in its oar in the form of OSHA regulations and procurement standards, as well as state and local requirements. On top of all of this are the corporations' own internal standards, as well as customs and concepts that the companies have lived with for many years.

The philosophical and conceptual bond that ties all of this together is, at best, very weak. The standards groups have been attempting for some time to put together a rationale for standards, usually based on some quantifiable metric. Several studies have been published purporting to show that standardization makes economic sense and that any rational-economic person should follow this path. Yet, the standards committees would be hard-pressed to find people who participate on their voluntary committees with purely rational-economic expectations. Standards committees seem bent on justifying their existences by using hard data to prove that standards are good, yet they persist in using altruistic appeals to attract committee members.

Conclusion

Standards represent different things to groups and disciplines, to organizations, and to individuals, and these meanings vary with time and context. The disagreement between the organizational and individual rationales and goals for participation in standardization is a major cause of confusion about standards and standardization in the IT industry. Just as there is no single, consistent body of literature that ties the individual to the system, there is no theoretical (or philosophical) basis for organizational development or participation. There is no unanimity on individual motivations for doing standards, nor on why people participate of their own free will in an arena that has only the most "macro" rationale for its existence. The common thread in the IT industry is a certain understanding of the major disciplines of the craft. If a commonality exists in its standards, it appears to derive from the shared experiences and expectations of the industry, not from the innate characteristics of the standards process. I believe that this may be due, in part, to ignorance of the background of standards and their moderately rich heritage. Without an understanding of standards as a separate discipline and market in themselves and not as a by-product of other processes, each new venture is pursued in isolation (or at least semi-isolation), re-creating the successes—and failures—of the past.

2. A SHORT HISTORY

OF STANDARDS

Standards, like the poor, have always been with us. Deliberately or inadvertently, they exist and have been used to control and organize much of humankind's activities. They are a powerful tool to stabilize and then promote exchange and growth, and they can also, if misused, cause a culture to stagnate and wither.

In their broadest sense, standards represent the acceptable behavior and mores of a society and culture. Language, for example, may be considered a standard, as could most of the activities that societies use to structure their existences, although this usually is not made explicit. In many cases, these cultural standards are derivative, generalized from some other function as part of the acculturation process.

In a more confined sense, *a standard is the deliberate acceptance by a group of people having common interests or background of a quantifiable metric that influences their behavior and activities by permitting a common interchange.* One of the first standards that meets the test of this definition is the establishment of a guaranteed national coinage that is respected by more than a single locality. The Lydian *stater*, minted with a guarantee of value, was the first coin created with the intent of encouraging trade, and it became a standard unit of exchange, accepted and recognized throughout the Mediterranean. Key to the importance of Lydian coinage was that it could be used to compare things in the abstract—that is, the value of two disparate things could be established by comparison to the *stater*. With a quantifiable common denominator to provide a basis for comparison and interchange, it became easier to get on with the business of trade—in other words, there was an economic advantage to be gained from using the standard. While it was probably much easier to calculate value in "proprietary" local currency, a standard currency increased both the potential of and area for trade. Pricing to a standard involved extra risk and work (the conversion process), but the potential for profit was greater than the potential loss.

From 500 B.C. to A.D. 500 practical, implemented standards stayed in fashion, especially in commerce. Trade grew, as did the need for standards to make it easier and more profitable. However, there was apparently little standardization of finished manufactured products; each manufacturer verified the quality of goods used, but nothing indicated the quality of outgoing goods, other than the reputation of the maker. Furthermore, since the concept of interchangeable parts had not yet gained popularity, the need for product standardization was minimal.

With the fall of the Western Roman Empire, European civilization took a gigantic step into isolationism, and commercial standards were lost for the next four hundred years. In the Byzantine Roman Empire, however, standards —internal and external—proliferated. Usually imperial decrees backed by the bureaucracy of Constantinople, these standards, for everything from weight to craftsman responsibilities, were the forebears of modern regulatory standards; nonetheless, they could be used for increasing commerce or exchange.

Meanwhile, back in Europe, commerce began to revive as agriculture grew above the subsistence level, leading to the growth of cities and the rediscovery of trade. It become essential to regulate the output of the craftsmen, out of economic necessity as much as civic pride. Cities became famous for a single product, which became the standard against which others were judged. Yet again, trade drove the establishment of standards.

Trade is not an end in and of itself, however, but a method to increase wealth. In Medieval Europe, the individual merchants belonged to craft guilds that established standards to maintain product quality, which was indicated by their hallmarks. Because it was in the interests of the towns to have wealthy citizens, the local civil authorities enforced guild trading rules. And because trade was taxable, the larger civil authorities promulgated rules to encourage its growth.

The object of standardization begins to appear clearly here: interchange is valued because it has economic value, not for its own sake. Max Weber, in *The Protestant Ethic and the Spirit of Capitalism*, notes that the development of a regulated set of expectations was one of the factors that encouraged the growth of structured capitalism. And, indeed, it was the development of formal rules—among them, standards—that fostered the calculated capitalism that marked European growth beginning in the 1500s.

Standards became more necessary as the nascent nation-states grew increasingly interdependent and the advent of the Industrial Revolution required more and more production in less and less time. Standards—both internal and external—became necessary to ensure that growth was not random and that a degree of commonality existed among nations. With the arrival of the era of interchangeability, standards increased in importance and became based more in functional definition and utility. Time itself was standardized, and other standards began to be predicated upon demonstrable scientific principles (Fahrenheit or Celsius, the metric system), with the decimal numbering system replacing other numbering systems. Decimal currency made its appearance in most major trading countries.

Finally, there was the invention of the railroad, which had a profound impact on the world. A substantial technical achievement, it also marked a major social and cultural milestone. Dispersion and distance no longer were impediments to trade; rather, they became positive allies. Railroads themselves used standards, since interchangeability of specially crafted machined parts was essential. The standardization of rail gauges in the United States often is pointed to as a major victory for standardization. (Unloading and reloading rail cars each time the gauge changed was tiresome and slow. For this reason, the gauges of rail lines in Europe changed at every border. An invading army, delayed for six to ten hours at a rail head, is an ideal target for attack, since it is usually bunched up and not formed for battle.)

River transport, the predecessor of the rail, did not require such standardization; railroads, however, could run where barges could not, encouraging dispersion of both supplies and products. This increased the demand and need for standards—an influence that has often been overlooked. Standardization becomes very important in a dispersed market, since it allows services or products to be replicated or repaired even at great distances from the original source. Maintainability, duplicability, and interchangeability constitute the three-part justification for standards from a consumer's viewpoint.

More and more things were standardized as the rail made possible increased industrialization. Industrialization, in turn, demanded ever more standards to maintain itself—standards in metallurgy, standards in information representation, in work units, in fasteners, in terminology, in education, in nearly every aspect of life.

The regulation in the United States

For the first hundred years of the United States' existence, regulations were the right and responsibility of the individual states, which imposed them to protect the common good of their citizenry. Regulations covered grist mills and gins, ferry crossings and highways, and sundry other activities necessary to the distribution of foodstuffs and to agricultural commerce in general. Few regulations were technically driven, since much of the technology, most of the products, and most practices were traditional. The advent of the steam locomotive required certain adjustments, but these regulations dealt with safety issues raised by the new technology, not with the technology itself. By and large, regulations were imposed locally at a state level, based on traditional learning and reflecting a relatively static civilization.

Following the Civil War, however, industrialization came in to its own; with it came abuse, as industry began its quest for profit and power. By the mid-1870s, a fundamental change had occurred in the society of the United States—the commercial interdependence of the various sections of the country became more and more pronounced and the need to sell over large geographical areas became dominant. Sears and Roebuck and Montgomery Ward took advantage of this change to establish mail-order stores in competition with local artisans, offering their merchandise as standards against which local merchants competed.

This growth, however, produced an unanticipated side effect. The concept of growth for profit's sake became increasingly popular—if big was good, large was better, and huge was spectacular—and the ability of the populace to protect itself against the ever-larger concentrations of economic and technical power began to decrease. The federal government, concerned (within limits) about the safety and welfare of its citizens, began to regulate commerce and other activities within its borders. It recognized that it could not regulate all aspects of industry, nor did it want to do so. Instead, it regulated those areas where the public and providers intersected and/or those in which the buyers could not evaluate the products that they purchased. Upton Sinclair's account of the meat-packing industry forced many changes, while Ida Tarbell's description of the Standard Oil Company did the same in an area that individuals or the various states could not control through lack of economic might. Cosmetics or railroads, boilers or power companies—anywhere the public good was threatened either by unwilling ignorance or by economic power, the government felt compelled to step in and regulate for the public good. *Caveat emptor* (Let the buyer beware) still applied, however; rather, the original phrase, *Caveat emptor quia ignorare non debuit quod jud alienum emit* (Let the buyer beware, because he should not be ignorant of the property that he is buying) continued to be the motto to live by.

Several facets of regulation should be mentioned here. First, what level of complexity can the consumer be expected to understand; in other words, when is it necessary to establish regulatory guidelines to delineate the responsibilities of both parties in a transaction? Second, regulations must be enforced, which creates adversarial relationships—who is the adversary and who the object of the government's protection? Third, regulations are ponderous; like a juggernaut, they are hard to start and steer, require vast throngs of people to keep them moving, and seem to acquire a life of their own once they get going—once rolling, they are usually difficult to stop. Finally, regulation, by its very nature, is specific to a single activity/occurrence. Global regulations cannot provide the necessary protection without also risking constant argument.

Inflexibility and calm majesty are inimical to a dynamic environment, in which change is an essential part of growth. Regulation responds by attempting to change the nature of change itself. If change is predictive and its course can be confined within guidelines, regulation can be applied intelligently. If, however, an unpredictable arena is regulated, the very act of regulation will introduce abnormalities into the environment, making it still more unpredictable. Regulations should not be used to cause or enforce social change; they are meant to regulate what already exists. If there is nothing to regulate or if the intention is to change a thing itself, a regulation is a poor tool.

Correctly applied, a regulation is a standards method that has the force of some authority behind it, a force that legitimately can compel use and exact a specified penalty for noncompliance. (The authority can be separated from the regulation; the regulation, however, constantly operates under the shadow of the legitimizing authority.) A voluntary consensus standard can be made into a regulation if a law enforcing its use is created; the original intent of the standard may be overlooked in these cases. In order to be effective, the regulation must be founded in rationality—either for the producer or the consumer—and enforceable, even on a group that may find it onerous. If the regulation is rational only to its creators and enforcers, it will likely be difficult to enforce, which may lead to yet more regulations. Ultimately, of course, there must be some benefit to the regulated, whether this is initially apparent or not. If it offers no benefit, the regulation is not only useless but counterproductive. Obviously, the more adversarial a relationship, the more regulators are needed. Yet, if a relationship is friendly, enforcement of the regulation may suffer.

Most of the regulations imposed by the government were not too onerous at their inception. Minor problems usually were prevented from becoming major; usually, the regulation was founded upon a collective body of wisdom. State and local regulations usually preceded the national efforts. These regulations, reflecting the experience and knowledge of their originators, were based upon local expectations and conditions and usually were reasonable within the context and time of creation. However, they suffered nonetheless from the faults noted above, tending, over time, to become more of an obstacle to change than a positive influence on industry.

The most ambitious piece of social regulation ever attempted was the Occupational Safety and Health Act (OSHA). This massive list of regulations was partially successful in accomplishing its task of promoting safety in the workplace. It was also, however, successful in ultimately weakening the will of the federal government to regulate, since the regulations were so global and numerous as to vitiate the ability and desire to enforce them, and compliance, at times, became absurd. OSHA may have made the workplace safer in the near term, but it also highlighted the absolute folly of trying to regulate an entire nation's industry. The outcome of OSHA may be the gradual dismantling of the large-scale regulatory capability of the federal government, defaulting to the regulatory capabilities of the states, under federal guidelines. By this, I do not mean to imply that federal regulation will ever disappear. Where there are dominant safety concerns (nuclear power, air traffic), where issues are too large to be handled by a single state (environmental issues, economic issues), or where processes are too complex to be widely understood (food and drugs, some process industries), regulations must and will continue. But the day of the well-intentioned regulation appears to be waning. Regulation is a poor substitute for market action in either a dynamic society or a dynamic industry: regulation in a dynamic industry in a dynamic society can be positively destructive, for both the regulated and the regulators.

Voluntary standards groups

Any cooperative joining to bring about the acceptance of a common thought or practice can be labeled a voluntary standards organization—although the group must have formal recognition from someone other than itself and must receive the approbation and acceptance of the society that its standards affect. The purpose of voluntary standards is not to mandate change but to cause the market to prefer a standard solution to a nonstandard solution. The entire process, from the initiation of the proposed standard through its publication, depends on freedom of choice and action—there is no intrinsic benefit attached to participation, nor is there a definite penalty attached to rejection.

Industry acceptance of common interests has been relatively widespread throughout history—the specialization of the wine-producing regions in France, Italy, and Germany is a fine example of the ability of people to use a standard to promote their economic interests. However, nonagricultural standards for more than local use had to wait for a compelling need. This, as noted above, was supplied by the Industrial Revolution and the increased demand for products of all kinds and fueled by the railroad and the Civil War, which forced a greater use of mechanization on the remaining artisans, as well as the farmers.

It was the secondary suppliers who most spurred the growth of voluntary standards. Screw sizes, pipe and valve fittings, and rail ties were just a few of the scores of newly standardized objects. Various interest groups coalesced within industries to ensure that their industry had its standards. Each organization was industry specific—no attempt was made to standardize outside of the industry or for the good of the customer. Standardization was intended to make the industry grow or to make it more profitable and/or less complex.

Standardization was pushed by the growing group of technocrats, headed by the engineers—civil, metallurgical, mining, electrical. For the first time, an emerging discipline had a body of literature that dealt with demonstrable reality, capable of being duplicated. The engineers of the second half of the nineteenth century created an open collection of scientific fact that supported their activities—a collection that was growing and could, in their minds, be applied to anything, from humans to metallurgy.

This reliance on a factual, demonstrable base is the hallmark of the standards industry—it is no accident that, in the late 1800s, the American Society for Testing and Materials (ASTM) was one of the first organizations to gain prominence as a standards group. And the extent to which these engineers tried to standardize often goes unnoticed; for example, the first major school of standardized management thought was developed under the aegis of the American Society of Mechanical Engineers, of which Frederick Taylor, the "Father of Scientific Management," was a member, along with many other early management pioneers.

The tone for the entire voluntary standards effort was set by 1890. There was the strong concentration on creating standards within specific disciplines (metallurgy, mechanical engineering, electrical engineering, etc.), an emphasis on demonstrable and reproducible facts, and an internal focus on the part of the participants—a modified siege mentality. These three attributes continue to this day. Each discipline has its standards committee, and several have quite a few. The emphasis is on creating hard products or standards that can be tested and duplicated, and each group is inwardly focused, composed of the developers and producers of the specific discipline. There is no place in the voluntary standards community for vague theories; all work must be based on fact and be capable of being described in unambiguous terms, with an outcome that is certain. Only recently did philosophic models evolve in IT standards. Their acceptance is slow, but the need for basic understanding is beginning to outweigh the need to quantify.

The purpose of these voluntary standards is not to mandate change but to cause the market to prefer a standard solution to a nonstandard solution. The entire process, from the initiation of the proposed standard through its publication, depends upon freedom of choice and action—there is no intrinsic benefit attached to participation, nor is there a definite penalty attached to rejection.

Conclusion

Table 2-1 lists some of the major differences between regulatory and voluntary standards. Clearly, each method has its virtues and vices, although which is which is a matter of personal judgment. The voluntary method appears to be more appropriate to standards activities in volatile areas with competing technological and application solutions available, where there are intense user and provider dynamics. While the voluntary method is slower, it accommodates more input and garners a larger base of support for completed standards. It also prevents single interests from dominating the standardization effort for self-serving ends. Regulatory standards, on the other hand, are more useful when there is only a single acceptable solution to a problem. They are usually more restrictive and do not furnish alternatives, since their purpose is to regulate specific activities, rather than to encourage growth or provide options.

Both methods, however, see the same benefits in standards: interchangeability, convenience, ease of use, interconnectability, safety, risk reduction, integration of technological improvement, and so on. The demand for these attributes is market driven; it did not spring into being full grown, like Athena from the head of Zeus. Safety regulations, for example, were driven by the government in response to demands from an outraged population when faced with a lack of

Table 2-1. A comparison of regulatory and voluntary standards

Standard type	Strengths	Weaknesses
Voluntary	Industry (group) support	No enforcement mechanism
	Market (user) driven	Lengthy process for resolution of conflict
	Originator must be skilled in understanding strategy and user needs	Strategic planning more difficult
	Opportunities to work outside of standards for new innovations	Commonsense interpretations necessary, which vary with application
Regulatory	Everyone must adhere to clear standard	No innovative flexibility in dealing with dynamic market
	Noncompliance with standard is immediately obvious	Precisely written, detailed standards must cover all possible situations
	Penalties and rewards for process compliance can be specified exactly	Litigation is common, stemming from disagreements over definitions or interpretations
	Implementation process for correctly written standard is clear	Source of standard must be an expert in all potential applications of standard to avoid limiting innovation
	Centralization of process is easier	Larger police force necessary to ensure conformity to standard
	Control is more complete	Compliance is mandatory, potentially arousing hostility in innovative groups

commitment on the part of producers to provide safe products. If there is a need in the market—usually driven by economics—the market will respond to that pressure.

Still, whatever the causes, people have accepted that standards and what they provide are good; by and large, no one questions their value. It is at this point that many standards groups have stopped evolving—finding out why is one of the more serious endeavors of this book.

3 . TOWARD AN EXPANDED DEFINITION OF CONSENSUS STANDARDS

> In front, the sun climbs slow, how slowly,
> But westward, look, the land is bright!
> *Say not the struggle naught availeth*
> Arthur Hugh Clough

Nearly all of the writings on standards of which I am aware have been based on a distinct standard or have been focused on a particular standards area. Nearly all examine standardization from the viewpoint of a particular discipline (engineering, communications, medicine, steel). It is not surprising that writers prefer to study the unfamiliar subject of standardization within the context of their specialties, but this approach has led them to overlook the concept of standards as an entity in and of themselves. This is not entirely their fault; editorial pressures contribute as well, since it is very difficult to cram a complete philosophy and explication of standards into twenty-one column inches in the technical press. Furthermore, the subject of standards tends to be as dry as a stick, for the most part.

This lack of length and depth does not matter for most popular articles in information technology. A byte is a byte (within limits), and other commonly used, applied, and understood terms and concepts serve as a form of shorthand. Most scientific disciplines seem to share this advantage. Disagreements can arise, but a common vocabulary and pool of experience eliminate the need to provide extensive background information in initial discussions. Standards, on the other hand, suffer from a twofold problem that does not afflict the world of IT. First, each standard relies on an interpretation of what is supposed to be the essential quality of the object being described, and interpretations vary depending on the person doing the describing. Second, standards must use nonquantifiable terms for these already vague descriptions.

There is no universal prescription that provides a way around the problem. The ultimate consumers of standards are individuals, each with a unique set of expectations and aspirations, which must also be viewed in light of national, regional, technical, and educational background and corporate or user affiliation. But the ambiguity caused by using the word "standards" to refer to all of the different types of standards that exist can be corrected with a typology of standards.

Major distinctions were made between regulatory and voluntary consensus standards in the previous chapter. A review of the various forms of consensus standards is now necessary. In the IT realm, consensus standards themselves are evolving as the information technology market continues to mature and expand.

Toward a typology of consensus standards

Within the current context of consensus standards organizations, all standards, once undertaken, are believed to have equal importance to the market. This has proven to be manifestly untrue, since standards can and do vary in importance to industry, user, and provider. There is the implementation standard (a standard used to implement a particular device) as opposed to the conceptual standard. In addition, there is a growing realization that some standards are process standards, while others are product standards.

These three aspects of standards—importance, conceptual versus implementation, and process versus product—intermix to produce interesting challenges for the consensus standards process. Removing them from their contextual settings will allow examination, definition, and validation. I propose to begin the examination with the most straightforward of the three—importance.

Importance

Within the information technology industry, the rift between users and providers has widened in the past several years, as users come to expect providers to fulfill the promises that they have made over the last decade. In many cases, expectations have been raised by the marketing of a particular solution. The notion of the "Office of the Future," with its miles of interconnecting cables over which all things communicate, has enormous appeal for the user. The constant mentions of the benefits of the interconnectability of system components and of user-friendly software that even a child can operate have set user expectations sky-high. From the wind planted by such campaigns, the industry is now beginning to reap the whirlwind: COS, MAP, TOP, and others demand that the vaunted interconnects be standardized, while from Germany have come proposed software ergonomic standards that would permit the novice user to experience the thrill of "programming" without first having to learn the subject. Additionally, in the quest for efficiency and optimization of increasingly expensive computer resources, many users have turned to standards as the solution to the incompatibility problems that now plague—and will continue to plague—the industry.

In both of these cases—keeping promises and optimizing resources—the concept of importance, measured by a dollar impact in both the users' and providers' worlds, is relevant. For the users, it is the cost of time *before* implementation of a standard; for the providers, it is the cost of the implementation itself. This difference in metrics is becoming critical as the pace of change accelerates and the level and intensity of disagreement between and among the users and providers grows. Some providers view standards as a threat to their economic well-being, believing that the longer they have the best unique solution, the more they stand to profit; others feel that the longer they do not have access to a specific technology contained in a proposed standard, the worse off they are economically. Users, on the other hand, may see a delay in standardization as a deliberate attempt by the providers to force single-vendor solutions; conversely, some believe that providers use standards to bring everyone down to a common level that can then be regulated by the providers. All of these divergent views must not be ignored; they are endorsed actively and cannot be changed without great effort.

Also varying from user to user and from provider to provider is the relative importance assigned to each particular activity. A standard that is very important to a specialized industry niche may have no overwhelming importance for the majority of standards participants, yet this standard is required to undergo the same process as a standard of major importance to the future of the entire industry. The consensus process does not factor importance into its procedure; each standard is accorded the same right to the process as any other. Even so, if the proponents of the niche standard believe that their vital need is not being expedited, they will blame the bureaucratic standards process.

Finally, a great deal of importance may be assigned to a standard for the wrong reason. If a standard is required to solve a problem that users failed to anticipate or a corporate management ignored, it has a high potential for failure or, at least, for a short life span. Standards cannot fill a gap caused by lack of managerial planning and foresight; instead, because of the nature of the consensus system, they are somewhat predictive and future oriented. Standards created to solve present problems usually create substantial future problems.

Implementation and conceptual standards

A standard, as a standard, can be envisaged as a plan that represents the proposed activities of the industry in dealing with an issue. However the issue is viewed by the participants, the standard should represent the industry response to a real problem, and, assuming that the problem was analyzed correctly, the standard should provide a valid solution. If the problem requires a sweeping solution, the standard should not confine itself to only a specific aspect of the problem, nor should a more modest problem invoke industrywide change as part of a solution. To cite conventional wisdom: Let the punishment fit the crime.

However, if one accepts the concept that a standard is the written solution to a future industry problem, then, by implication, standards committees are acting to steer the industry. There are three distinct categories into which such standards-creation activities can fall: (1) standards that plan to change the industry; (2) standards that reinforce existing industry patterns; and (3) standards that cause unplanned change. Standards that plan to change the industry are usually conceptual; standards that reinforce existing industry patterns usually relate to implementation; standards that cause unplanned change can fall into either the conceptual or the implementation category.

Because the information technology industry is dynamic, solutions must evolve with the problems they solve. An implementation standard is intended to ensure that the evolution of an answer keeps slightly ahead of the evolution of the question. An example is the COBOL standard, which changes so that COBOL remains responsive to the current and future needs of the industry. While the standard is new at each revision, the solution it provides—a business-oriented language that can be used widely, has stability, and is easily implemented—does not change but rather evolves to meet the changing needs of those who demanded it in the first place. Accredited Standards Committee (ASC) X3J4 (the standards committee responsible for COBOL) makes sure that changes to COBOL are implemented in a manner that is evolutionary rather than revolutionary. The intent is to reinforce the activities of the industry, not to change them.

Implementation standards groups are not automatically noncontentious, however. The term "implementation" refers only to the nature of the problem being considered; it does not reflect unanimity on the part of the participants in the process. In any collection of independent people, different opinions on changes abound and are held dear.

Changing people's minds can take time and energy, yet the process must proceed, if the goal is to arrive at a true consensus standard that will respond to the future needs of the industry.

If the implementation standards are seen as evolutionary, then conceptual standards are revolutionary, seeking to change industry perceptions and direction, to encourage technology conversion or change, or to redefine an industry problem through a different perspective on the approach to a solution (usually technologically based) or a different perspective on the problem itself. Creation of these standards, usually driven by an individual or a provider, takes an immense amount of patience, time, and effort on the part of the participants, since deliberate change is difficult to introduce.

One well-known conceptual standard is the IEEE 802.3 Ethernet standard, initiated in response to a perceived market need to provide separate users access to computing facilities without degrading user performance or duplicating the centralized resources. Whether to distribute resources or degrade performance had been viewed as a trade-off—distributed resources provided high performance at expense, and centralized resources provided low cost with degraded performance. The developers of Ethernet redefined the problem, focusing on communications between the user and the systems resources. By concentrating efforts in this area, the concept of the Local Area Network (LAN) was developed, leading to a revolution in the way that computers were conceptualized and structured. As the Ethernet standard continued to develop, abrupt shifts in the design and use of IT equipment occurred, exceeding the original expectations of the LAN developers. While the LAN could be called a natural progression of technology, it provided a starting point from which other technologies could grow, allowing providers and users alike to focus their energies, efforts, and activities on providing further solutions, instead of defining and redefining the same old problem.

Any standard, once initiated, may cause unplanned change. This usually happens because someone outside a standards committee sees an opportunity to use the standard in a way that the group drafting the standard has failed to see. This happened to ASC X3T9.5, which is concerned with providing a high-speed interface between CPUs and their mass storage devices. The committee originally had proposed the Local Distributed Data Interchange (LDDI) as an implementation standard to provide an elegant technical solution to a growing, but understood, problem—how to connect a CPU to mass storage or to another CPU in the face of the rising costs of interconnect and the increasing need to transmit data more quickly and safely than was provided by current standards. The LDDI was an implementation standard because it was codifying an existing idea and used a strategy of congruence because it was an extension of a known industry solution.

ASC X3T9.5 then began work on the Fiber Optic Distributed Data Interchange (FDDI), also as an implementation standard, which modified the work in LDDI by substituting glass for copper. The solution was driven partially by technology (fiber is newer and therefore more "fun" than copper) and partially by an effort to meet the longer term needs of the industry by providing still more capacity for the transmission of data (fiber has a substantially higher transmission capability than does copper). The solution was well suited to the problem and would have met all of its developers' expectations, except for one small problem: the committee had overlooked the fact that application of fiber was in its early stages in the IT industry. As the industry began to recognize the potential in fiber optics, the expected uses for it began to multiply, and the work of the FDDI committee became responsible for changing the way people looked at interconnects. This shift was not deliberate; it just happened. The standard, when completed, will fulfill the intentions of its developers by describing the necessary methods for connecting fiber-optic cable to mass storage and to CPUs—but the industry will use this connection to do things envisioned by neither the committee nor the industry when the process was started.

Product and process standards

The rate of technological change in the IT industry is increasing. This acceleration exerts two major pressures on the consensus standards process. The first of these is the collapsing life cycle of most IT products worldwide; the product life expectancy has decreased from ten to five years and may decline yet again. The functions that the products perform are not changing, but the ever greater demands for more speed, more performance, more reliability, and less space—to mention just a few—can be met only by more and more innovative engineering, products, and applications.

The second stress derives from the nature of the consensus standards process itself. It is not a quick process, nor is it meant to be. Consensus does not mean majority agreement; it indicates that a commonality of perception and opinions has been achieved. To gain consensus, there must be time to resolve disputes, not by compromise, which gives all parties a partial victory and a partial defeat, but by redefining the problem so that it lends itself to a solution that will meet the needs of all participants. The process takes time and effort: when there is no one right answer, arguments can become dogmatic because of economic, personal, or regulatory need. Once a problem has been redefined, however, a new answer that can and does satisfy the participants can be worked out, but this, too, takes time.

To mitigate the pressure of change, a new form of standard is becoming more and more common: the *process* standard, as opposed to the *product* standard.

A product standard describes a product or service being standardized. The product, which should have a future orientation (although this is not an absolute necessity), defines the standard in that the standard merely exists to serve as a paradigm for the product within the industry. In other words, the standard and the product/service being described are equivalent within the confines of a single discipline/structure, free of external dependencies. The standard assumes that the external interfaces to the product it describes are relatively constant and consistent. Although a product standard can accept a wide variability of inputs if the standard specifies the variability, it usually is constructed rather tightly; if a standard calls for a series of options, which can be implemented randomly in terms of numbers, sequences, and fashions, then its purpose is defeated. Since, by definition, the consensus process must somehow include all opinions perceived as necessary or have a satisfactory reason for rejecting them, it is very easy for a product standard to become so generalized or so complex that it is no longer viable.

The process standard focuses on the transmutation of a customer need into a customer solution, examining a system's inputs and outputs but not concerning itself especially with the products that accomplish the transmutation. In other words, it is concerned with the ends, not means. For example, if a process standard is intended to standardize the transmission of information, it addresses whether or not the information is transmitted and usable when it is received and not how the transmission is achieved. This concept has substantial implications for the development of standards, because it is device independent; rather than specifying a certain product or service to meet a need, it merely describes the need, the constraints to achieving the solution, and the output necessary to allow the results of the standardized solution to interplay with solutions from other process standards.

If a standard represents a future-oriented response by industry to a perceived problem, then the process described in the standard must also be future oriented. Knowledge of problem definition and solution and awareness of the implications for the future that the process implies and actualizes are both vitally necessary. Furthermore, process standards are a function and result of their context: problems or user needs do not exist in isolation; they must come from somewhere. It is this aspect—the context—that becomes most critical, posing the greatest challenge in consensus standards development. The challenge lies not in the description of the process outcome—the systematic solution to the need—but in the accurate reading of the user need and then in the determination of the process description. An improper reading of a need can lead to a completely unsuitable process standard, and even a successful description of a need does not guarantee the successful description of the solution.

For example, describing a process correctly based on an incorrect or inaccurate understanding of the need can lead either to indifference or to confusion on the part of the market, neither of which is healthy to the consensus process. Indifference would follow the creation of a standard, under consensus, that misleads the market by causing it to misdirect its energies, by providing a solution to a nonexistent problem, or by providing a nonsolution to an existing problem.

Market confusion has even more substantial implications, which extend beyond the arena of standards. If the market is only confused, it will cast about among the alternatives available and, eventually, using Adam Smith's "invisible hand," select one that appears to be valid: it loses only time and, sometimes, a sense of purpose. A much more serious impact can occur, however, if the industry is heavily technology driven or influenced. Improperly applied process standards can trap the industry in an obsolete technology or divert it from the main course of technology. In this case, the industry must find the correct technology for its uses, redefine its purpose, and then restart to accomplish the new, or redefined, purpose. This can be especially difficult if the industry had been certain that it was doing the right thing previously and, in fact, had been following the tenets advocated by an accepted standard. Having lost faith in itself and, therefore, in its own correctness of perception, the industry may act randomly, which may lead to multiple technologies, causing the market to splinter and lose the coherence that sometimes adds strength to technology.

The distinctions between product and process standards apply primarily to dynamic markets. In a static market, if the interrelationships between products are constant or if the pace of technological change is slow, product standards will subsume process standards. The product, in order to function, must fit into the larger process correctly; if it does not, both product and process will fail, because the desired result and the tool to produce it are not compatible. In the case of a correctly written and structured product standard that fits into the market, the process is inferrable from the product. If the process described in the standard is containing steam to increase pressure and temperature and the product described is a boiler, the process and product are equivalent: one could deduce from the boiler standard the process that it is intended to carry out. (The reverse, however, is not true.) If the market is dynamic, however, a product may be made obsolete by changes in the demands and requirements of the process, which do not diminish the essential validity of the process but do affect the way it is accomplished.

Reunification

Of the three aspects of consensus standards that I have described, importance is a factor in all cases. The others—implementation versus conceptual and product versus process—can be combined in various ways to produce several very different kinds of standards. There are four possible valid combinations: implementation/product, implementation/process, conceptual/product, and conceptual/process.

Most common is the implementation/product standard, which deals with an established product or service, with known rules and boundaries, that is being updated for use in a changed or changing environment or is being used to formalize a response to a known, existing, and ongoing market need. In keeping with the need for future orientation that was postulated in the last section, the product is assumed to be capable of being modified for use in the changing environment or the requirement is stated in such a way that the proposed standard solution will not become obsolete quickly. If the product or service being standardized is a response to a market need that is no longer valid, the standard-making/-modifying activities are valuable only for historical reasons or for reasons other than those that normally apply to standards.

Like any implementation standard, the implementation/product standard is best used in areas where there is a consensus on user and market needs and expectations, which are bounded and clearly user defined. Although the market that uses this type of standard is dynamic, I believe that it is safe to state that it has an aura of predictability. The creation of any standard can be hectic, sometimes bordering on the frenetic, but the motive behind the creation of an implementation/product standard often is prosaic and calmly stated. These standards are intended to service a predictable market with a predictable response.

The implementation/process standard is more difficult to categorize. The two adjectives seem almost incompatible, since the concept of process has more future-oriented, global implications than does that of implementation. Yet both must be accommodated in situations where a well-established need, too complex or too simple to be met by a single product, requires a standard that is not bound to a single technology or methodology. This would be the case in the standardization of a system, where the results of the system are known and expected by the industry and the market as a whole is not especially concerned about the methods used to achieve them. Whether the market need—and the process that satisfies it—is complex or simple, the standard should describe the process of obtaining the expected result, not the product that produces it.

The most obvious illustration of the implementation/process standard is the telephone system, in which users are very concerned with the user interface that they see and use—the conventional ten digits, dialing conventions, and voice transmission—but really don't care about the technology employed to achieve communication. The well-established need exists—to communicate by voice over distance—and the users want this need satisfied; methodology takes second place to results.

Conceptual/product standards are already relatively widespread in the information technology industry, which is very dynamic and has a tendency to be product, not process, driven. This type of standard also is appearing more and more frequently in the general population of standards, as technology forces changes in the materials use and fabrication industries. When a new technology is being implemented, a conceptual/product standard assures the market that its perceptions are valid—through it, the market reaffirms its own correctness. This type of standard usually relates to a product or service with a technical or marketing variation about which the users or providers are unsure. Because safety is perceived in numbers, the call for a standard based on a future product becomes very strong.

Reaffirmation of a collective need (and the collective response to the need) is one of the more important functions of the consensus standards process. If a proposal for a standard generates no interest except among a small group of proponents, they must ask whether the conceptual product is a valid response to a market need. If no one is interested in working to develop the standard, the odds are that the concept is of little interest to the industry at large and that no one will endorse the resultant product. The need for the standard becomes moot, since innovation for innovation's sake is not encouraged by the market, most individuals, and society in general. However imperfectly, the consensus standards process helps the market determine when innovation is frivolous and when it serves a purpose, by providing a neutral arena where the impacted community as a whole safely can question, advocate, argue, and generally explore an innovative approach.

The die-hard advocate risks the most in this process, since she/he must justify the change and show positive results that outweigh its cost. The other option, of course, would be to pursue the proposal as a proprietary response to the market, choosing to believe that the proposed solution is correct and conventional wisdom mistaken. Usually, this fails. But when it does succeed, it can pay large and impressive dividends to the visionaries (the technical term for those who succeed by flouting the market).

One of the factors helping to increase the number of standards in this category is the movement away from the use of consensus standards as a substitute for regulations, caused by the growing awareness that conceptual/product standards do not describe an implemented product, but rather are future oriented and marketing driven, both forces inimical to the regulatory use of standards. The conceptual/ product standard has the potential for becoming an important part of the advanced development process as companies begin to respond to the foreshortening of the product life cycle. Unfortunately, because only a handful of people in the industry are aware that the success of the consensus process depends on at least three general reviews, which are built into the process and take a significant amount of time, there is an increasing pressure to quicken the pace of conceptual/ product standardization.

Seeking to improve their chances of survival in an increasingly hostile market, many companies hope that their products can be standardized (read "approved by the standards bodies so that the market will accept them") after they have exited the development cycle. The problem here, of course, is that, within the constraints of the conceptual/product framework, the product should be offered to the market as a potential solution to a future problem, rather than as an immediate solution to a current problem. When a provider is asked to change a product or service to allow the needs of the market to be met more completely, there is a potential for conflict between the provider and the standards body (composed of provider and user peers) that is asking for the change.

The conceptual/product standard provides users with a reasonably good indication of where and how the industry as a whole is moving; to ignore such a standard, no matter how valid the reason, is perilous. However, users must also realize that the standards process describes future products, which are in the state of becoming, not of being. If a user builds an entire implementation on a preliminary proposal, only to have to scrap it when a provider changes the design to conform to a request from a standards committee, the resulting feeling of betrayal can be immense and, ultimately, destructive.

All of this is equally applicable to the conceptual/process standard, which also possesses its own unique complexities. A process standard is written to describe a set of expected events that will lead to a satisfactory set of outputs based on a specified set of inputs. A conceptual standard, however, is inherently mutable. Putting these two together yields a standard that describes an expected outcome for a future need. The risk is that, although the standard may meet all of the requirements for which it was intended originally, its creation may coincide with the development of an alternative process that obsoletes it completely. (The term "obsoletes" is used guardedly; if the input and output are provided in a fashion adequate to solve the perceived problem, the obsolescence will come because the competing process had decided advantages that the market believes are worthwhile.)

The conceptual/process standard is also extremely susceptible to semantic error. The process, by definition, must be somewhat vague, to allow technology and the market to change without obsoleting the standard, and the future orientation of the standard means that its description of a process must be even more hazy.

Four general types of standards, each with a specific functionality and rationale, have been postulated and examined. With the addition of importance (or user/provider context), however, the clarity disappears. Imagine a typical international standards meeting where work is being performed on a conceptual/process standard for the information technology industry. Assume a small meeting of approximately thirty representatives—say, twelve from providers, eight from government, five from impacted users or quasi-governmental bodies, several consultants, and a couple of academics. Then consider the national, regional, and international aspects of the meeting, the needs of the providers to ensure that their processes are not compromised, the governmental issues such as security and national prestige and protection of industry, and the academic section's insistence on a good and technologically sound solution. Finally, factor in the personal characteristics of the delegates, most of whom are highly competent engineers who have been working on this type of technological problem for years and for whom this arena is a chance to air their theories to their peers. Each individual represents herself/himself, an affiliated group (user, provider, government), a specific discipline (hardware, software, electrical engineering, computer science, marketing, legal), national and regional positions, and the specific company or user group that funded her/him at the meeting. It is easy to see why tidy definitions collapse in the face of so many different interests. As an aid to understanding the influence of these interests, several assumptions can be made about the participants in the process.

The most basic assumption is that everyone has a reason for participating. This does not necessarily mean that the reasons are positive; it is possible to participate in a standards meeting as a spoiler, attempting to slow or neutralize a standard so that a competing technology or process will prevail. Moreover, participants' motivations may be defensive or offensive. A participant may join in a particular standards effort, even though it contradicts professional beliefs, just to ensure that a potentially worse option is not adopted. Or the motivation may be to get the market to agree by means of a standard, which is what most standard bodies would prefer people to retain.

A second assumption is that, although the depth of belief and conviction will vary from individual to individual and from time to time, everyone who attends a meeting has an opinion about the subject under discussion—and will not necessarily express that opinion openly. Hidden agenda are a given at many meetings. Various levels of strategy are being executed during the conference, the meetings, dinners, and chance encounters. This is one of the major reasons why standards meetings are so important to the consensus process: they inject the element of human interaction, where deals are made, trades struck, and the participants come to understand the motivations and obligations that impel their peers to act as they do. Such understanding will not guarantee sympathy or support for the position taken, but the exposure, at least, may provide a measure of increased knowledge.

The final assumption is that the industry—users and providers alike—is more and more aware that standards are a serious business concern that can cripple or aid efforts to minimize exposure to the vagaries of the market. As this realization has grown, the composition of the standards groups has begun to change. Instead of coming from a regulatory or internal standards background, more and more representatives have a background in technical management. Perfect standards are no longer the goal; instead, the focus is on obtaining a workable and acceptable standard within a time frame that will allow it to be useful.

A definition of standards

Most definitions of standards describe the attributes of the specific standard or standards under immediate consideration, and I certainly have provided several such lists in my rather lengthy description of the individual types of standards. However, no list, no matter how exhaustive, truly can constitute a definition—attributes should flow from a definition, not the reverse. Thus, I propose to offer a new definition that will serve this purpose for standards. I begin with a behavioral definition of the attitudes and behaviors of the participants in the standardization process:

Standardization is the product of a personally held belief that the market has the ability to understand and chart a valid future direction through the use of collective wisdom, to understand the impact of change on itself, and to adjust itself to that change. The specific change agents utilized in this process are collective technical descriptions of how things ought to be and function, called standards.

From the understanding of the motivation of the participant (provider or user), further attributes and definitions can be developed:

A standard, of any form or type, represents a statement by its authors, who believe that their work will be understood, accepted, and implemented by the market. This belief is tempered by the under-

41

standing that the market will act in its own best interests, even if these do not coincide with the standard. A standard is also one of the agents used by the standardization process to bring about market change.

A corporation will accept and use standards only if it believes that it cannot control the market directly and that standards can. These two factors—acceptance of the market as externally controlled and understanding of the tools available to influence the market—determine when a firm is willing to participate in standards. This epiphany is not triggered by reaching any specified size, organizational typology, revenue, or other readily identifiable marker. The catalyst for using standards is external, residing in the mutable cultural setting in which the corporation must operate.

Individuals—whether separately or collectively—accept and use standards only if they believe that standards offer a benefit. This benefit usually is not distinct or quantifiable; rather, it is a trade-off of less desirable for more desirable factors. Many of these factors are defined subjectively and unconsciously, which makes their quantification extremely difficult, if not impossible. The factor that acts as the trigger for the individual may be less difficult to isolate than the corporate trigger, but this could be proven only by a case-by-case examination. It is far more difficult to generalize about individual triggers, however, since they sometimes can appear to be completely illogical.

The definition relies heavily on the concept of "the market" for its legitimacy. This dependence is justifiable if the term "market" is used to mean a collection of individuals outside of the control of the particular participant. Additional definitions come into play as well. "The market" is used in the most global sense here—it is not circumscribed by location (the Wall Street market), nor by company ("our market"), nor by individual (marketing/sales people). Rather, it denotes the large group of entities that uses some aspect of the IT industry when it needs to solve a problem. This market exists because unfilled and unanticipated needs arise, to which it responds. Its function is to provide a common ground where needs can be met and direction set.

Standards can come into play only when there are coordination problems between two or more entities. Ensuring coordination is relevant only when the parties recognize a problem with the coordination of their activities and are willing to attempt to solve it. Without the willingness to acknowledge a potential problem in coordination, to understand the implications of the problem, and to work toward a noncontentious solution, a consensus standard process cannot work nor a consensus standard develop.

The consensus standards process can be considered reasonably democratic; if equality among participants, at least in the proceedings, is denied, then the process must fail, since it is based on the belief that all parties can and will contribute something. They need not have equal expertise or resources, merely an equal right to utilize or abuse the process as they wish. It is true that, in many consensus standards committees within the information technology industry, the position and power of the participants derives, not from their corporate or user affiliation, but from their perceived competence with respect to the task at hand; the locus of power will shift as the meeting progresses, depending on what aspect of the standard is being discussed. Nonetheless, in nearly every case, all participants are heard when they wish to voice concerns on a particular topic.

The definition is very focused on the participants in the process. The reason for this should be relatively clear: the dynamics and attitudes that drive the standards process are heavily dependent on the rationale for the players' participation. But it also emphasizes the importance of the user interface, in a concept derived from William of Occam's Law of Parsimony: the most plausible standard will have the fewest newly invented interfaces for the user. In other words, the interface that is the most familiar to the user—in terms of expectations and preconceptions—probably will be the most well accepted and, hence, the most successful in the market. This is equally true of implementation (evolutionary) standards and conceptual (revolutionary) standards.

Testing the definition of standards against the aspects of standards used in the typology here (as well as others) creates no major problems; it even allows context to be a major factor. However, the definition is not predictive—it cannot describe when a standard is needed except by hindsight: if a standard appears and is successful, then its quality and the market need for it are obvious. This failing cannot be cited as a serious flaw, however, since it is not unique to the standards environment. It exists in all facets of business: there is no sure way to spot a winner.

4 . A NEW MODEL

FOR STANDARDS

> Yes! to this thought I hold with firm persistence;
> The last result of wisdom stamps it true:
> He only earns his freedom and existence,
> Who daily conquers them anew.
>
> *Faust*
> Johann Goethe

IT standards move from the abstract to the concrete, in that they describe systems that have not yet come into existence except in model or conceptual form. (These are the conceptual/product and conceptual/process standards.) Moreover, the IT industry is moving, in many cases, to standards that anticipate the actual creation of a product and are used to define a market, with all of its implications. The standards model, however, has not moved from the implementation/product model of standardization, where the implications of the thing being standardized do not need to be considered, since they are already known, to one that can deal with the new complexities caused by the anticipatory nature of standards. This is due, in part, to the nature of the standardization process, which traditionally operates from a concrete object to an abstraction of that object. The current model is predicated upon a simple two-stage approach that sees the standards process as a reactive activity that specifies something that already exists, often producing a formalized *de facto* standard that simply confirms what an industry already believes.

This model served the IT industry well through the early 1970s, when OEMs became an increasingly important part of the IT industry. As the role of these resellers of equipment grew, their ability to compete with manufacturers depended on their ability to provide solutions that the manufacturers could not. In many cases, these were software solutions, with their own niche applications; on occasion, though, the OEMs survived by providing systems that were the equivalent of the original providers', but at a lower cost. The need to price low drove many OEMs to create heterogeneous systems, since it was impracticable for them to mark down and resell manufacturers' complete systems. This need for heterogeneous systems created a need for interoperability from a hardware point of view. At the same time, the growth of plug-compatible computers offered another solution to the same problem—retention of software. Finally, as computers grew in importance, many users began to feel that major vendors were taking advantage of them, and there arose a demand for open systems.

But how was the interconnectability required by open systems to be achieved? Obviously, the leading provider or providers could not supply the methodology to the users, since this was exactly what they had been criticized for doing. As a result, standards were pressed into service to act as the method whereby provider independence would be achieved, since, in a standards committee, each provider and user had a single vote. It was democracy in action.

This approach produced two problems, however. One was the technical complexity of the interoperability concept. The other was the growth of the use of computing, especially in the late 1970s and the early 1980s, a growth not only in size but in application and the complexity of application. These two problems are responsible for the change in the perception of standards. Standardization—that is, the act of normalizing a thing or service—requires that both the technology and the application of the thing being standardized lend themselves to the process. In the 1970s and the 1980s (and continuing to the present), new applications for the technology and product/service of that technology appear each day. With each new application and each new technology, the older model of standardization became a little more difficult to apply and a little more difficult to accept.

Growth could be accommodated through one of two responses: expansion of a given standard to include more and more of the change or creation of more and more limited standards. Both approaches were tried simultaneously in the IT industry. Both worked—and the simultaneous implementation of both responses has been almost fatal to the standards program of the industry.

As an example of the first approach, the Open Systems Interconnect (OSI) standard describes in global terms the way that open systems should operate. However, it also specifies the complete spectrum of choices open to the market within its framework. Obviously, no provider or user could or even would implement all of the options provided, yet these options must be contained within the standard to encompass all of the possibilities of computing as it will be practiced when the standard is completed.

At the same time, each option in the standard comes with a price—measured either in performance, system complexity, or system size. For the user, who is trying to buy an interoperating system that meets business requirements, the global standard presents a problem. To make sense of the model, the user will specify the appropriate parts of the OSI standard, as well as the parts of all of the other standards that affect him or her—from quality of design to portability of assets. This specification process is costly, consuming expensive resources over time. In order to lessen the cost to each individual user, users in a particular industry will join together to provide common requirements documents, which will be called a standard as well—in this case, of the variety described in the second approach.

To complicate matters further, in IT standardization, users rarely participate on standards committees and are virtually absent from the accredited SDOs. The cost of participation is prohibitive for most users, but, perhaps more importantly, users tend to be less focused on long-term IT standards than they are on the use of standards to provide solutions to business problems, both current and future. As a result, they feel that the activities of the standards committees have little relevance to them.

It is critical to recognize that providers and users no longer have the same goals: the first group is the tool maker and the second the tool user. This analogy, however, is misleading: tool makers of yore understood the uses to which their tools would be put; the IT providers do not. They build their systems to meet a future capability, while the IT users design their responses to meet their own internally generated requirements. The IT world, and, by extension, IT standardization, has split into two camps—one polarized around the users and their interests in implementation and the other around the providers and their global concerns. The boundary that separates the two is not infrangible; that is, it does not prohibit the users from moving to the providers' side, nor does it prohibit the providers from being viewed as users. However, in the main, the providers of IT products and services must be seen as distinct from the users of IT products and services.

The different emphases of providers and users in standardization have, like the change in standardization described above, been overlooked. By and large, just as many continue to believe that a two-stage model of standardization is still applicable, many assume that one big happy (or at least not too quarrelsome) family is creating standards. I feel that it is time for a new model, one that recognizes the inaccuracy of both of these popular assumptions, understands the distinction between the two populations of the IT world, and acknowledges that standards are driven by the needs of business to provide some degree of predictability to that world. Most importantly, it must accommodate the two very different animals referred to as "standards" by providers and users.

On the provider side is the global model that describes all of the potentials that the IT industry will need if it is to satisfy all users over a long time in nearly all situations and that serves as a reference for all providers. This reference model, if it is correctly constructed, includes some present and future technologies, a road-map function, and some of the methodologies of the thought processes that occurred when it was constructed. The time span covered is up to ten years, and the model is applicable to all technical disciplines that deal with this area. On the IT user side is a description of a solution implementation that is immediate and particular to the problems of that user's application.

The first two distinct areas that must be covered by a new model have been identified. However, their differences in terms of time and complexity prevent them from having any but the slightest congruence, based as they are on different perceptions of the role of standards. If a single model is to serve for the entire industry, these two kinds of standards must meet on some common ground.

To begin, a subset of the reference model is necessary. The subset would possess the qualities of an industry consensus standard and typically would describe one set of functions or capabilities. That is, instead of a global reference model for Local Area Networks, the industry standard would describe a particular technological implementation of one LAN, such as Ethernet, specific to a single industry, such as IT. In effect, the industry standard is the implementation of the strategy contained in the reference model. Because the standard is written primarily by the providers of the product or service, it is more focused on a computing function—that is, on how the computing function will occur—than on its outcome. Little thought is given to the end use (application) here; instead, the various providers input market data through the selection of technologies. The providers create the standard in light of what they see as possible and viable—as well as needed. The providers act for the users in determining the course that the industry standard will take. Each provider represents its own users and makes implicit and explicit assumptions as to what they will need—collectively and individually—from the standard, when it is completed.

On the other side of the model, there is a need to generalize from the very specific implementation applications that describe what each particular user wants from the purchased system. The next level of generalization would be the systems profile, which describes the requirements of groups of similar users, based on a standardized set of needs for that group of users. As an example, a systems profile would contain a generalized description of the desired functionality, along with the methodology for ensuring that generality. The systems profile can be seen as an aggregate of a set of implementation applications—that is, a group of application implementation requirements would be combined to create the systems profile for a specific class or type of user. In order to agglomerate the requirements, however, one must be able to extrapolate a more generalized standard from a specific implementation of a particular standard. In such cases, user groups have been formed to write the standardized specifications upon which the users will base their individual implementation applications. These standardized specifications are the basis for the standards that form the systems profiles. In effect, the user group is putting together a list of requirements that providers must meet if the user is to be able to proceed to the implementation application.

Even with the addition of these two submodels, there is still no union of user and provider standards efforts. The industry standard is focused on the potentialities perceived by the provider industry; the systems profile defines the attributes on which a specific user group has standardized. The bridge between these two groups comes with the addition of the functional profile, which simultaneously describes a set of functions extracted from the industry standard and a set of functions required by a larger class of users than is represented in the more precise systems profile. In other words, it translates the potentiality of an industry's capabilities in a certain area into a set of functions from which users can begin to construct a more specific system. The functional profile exists in a limbo between provider perceptions and user needs, an area of uneasy cooperation where the providers discover if they have anticipated user needs correctly and users find out if what they need is within the scope of what the industry can provide. I believe that, in the future, most conflicts will occur in this area, which fortunately happens to be the area that offers the most room for compromise.

Figure 4-1 shows the five stages of the full model. Although it only provides the starting point for an attempt to deal with the complexities of the standardization process, the model's simple, logical represen-

Figure 4-1. Five-stage model for standardization

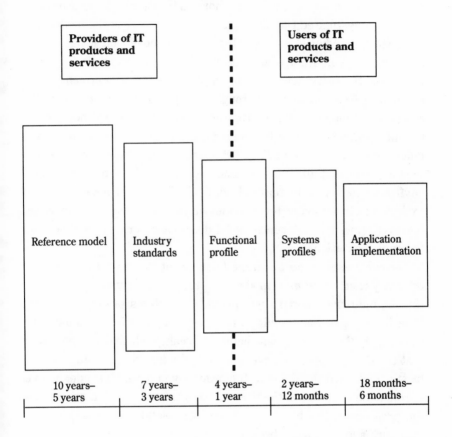

<table>
<tr><td>Providers of IT products and services</td><td></td><td>Users of IT products and services</td></tr>
</table>

| Reference model | Industry standards | Functional profile | Systems profiles | Application implementation |

| 10 years– 5 years | 7 years– 3 years | 4 years– 1 year | 2 years– 12 months | 18 months– 6 months |

tation of reality points to several areas that merit further study. To begin, it spotlights the time/event horizon in the standards process. I have not investigated the implications of this aspect of the model, and I am not sure what it implies. However, I believe that it has significance for the voluntary consensus standards process, since the event horizon of the reference model implies a ten-year commitment to see a standard from conception through to implementation. If this is the case, and I believe that it is, reference models likely will become the premier planning devices for the industry, acting as change agents to influence the evolution of IT. Furthermore, the possibility of revolution is somewhat diminished, since revolution in a highly planned environment will be increasingly difficult. This environment will not exclude the insertion of technologies or restrict technical innovation, however, since the reference model does not describe a methodology for implementation.

Second, despite the apparent linearity of the model, there is no certainty that a reference model will precede an industry standard or that an industry standard will precede a systems profile. While the time line is nice for planning purposes, very few users know what their needs will be ten years hence. In reality, all that can be said is that the market tends to develop eventually into the five-stage model; however, it need not do so in the order given here. This adds a level of confusion that makes the model somewhat suspect as a precise tool for prognostication but can enhance its usefulness as a means to structure and plan more broadly.

A final major complication becomes evident in Figure 4-2, which illustrates what happens to the model as it moves from the global to the specific. Each stage of the model becomes more particular, and, each time this happens, the original feature is subsetted as it is transferred to the lower level. The reference model can be implemented in several industry standards; each of these can be referenced in several functional profiles. Each functional profile can be subsetted to become part of several systems profiles, and each of these can be subsetted further as an implementation application.

Figure 4-2. The model from the provider's point of view

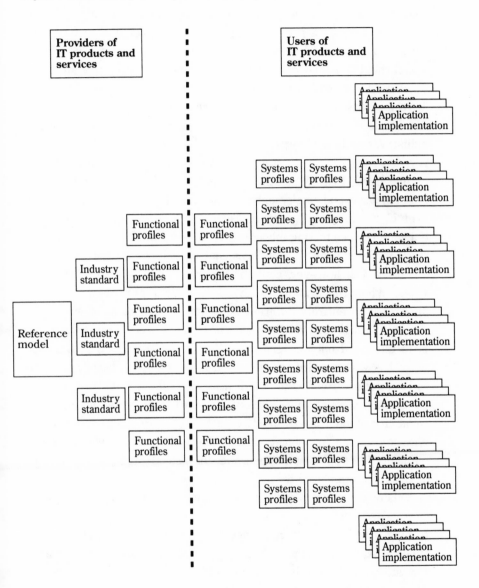

This does not present too great a challenge in most decompositions, since they are for static environments. However, in the case of standards, it becomes a major horror show very quickly. Standards are revised and updated constantly. Now, because they are no longer monolithic but rather can have several hundreds of interrelated sections and because they are updated as the originating committees see fit, the ability to determine the revision status of the various parts and levels of a standard begins to disappear. The levels below the industry standard never can be sure that they are using the latest revision of the industry standard. The ramifications of this problem extend beyond the difficulties of ensuring that the latest technology is being used and implemented. The immediate question is how, or even if, interoperability can be assured. At this time, I do not know if a conformance testing model can be built for the industry if the five-stage model is valid. It is an area that must be investigated.

Figure 4-2, however, contains a particular bias—that of the provider. When the graphic is reversed, as in Figure 4-3, the result illustrates an entirely different but equally valid point of view—the user's. Throughout this discussion, the user's need for standards has been discussed only in terms of IT. But the truth is that the user must deal with a multitude of standards—not merely those that relate to IT. IT standards, telecommunications standards, quality standards, governmental regulations, safety standards, service standards, and reliability standards—to mention just a few—are all part of the application implementation. So, from the user's point of view, the implementation application appears as the primary unit, into which all of the other standards feed.

This observation, more than any other, brings into focus the area of standards that most needs to be understood. While it is acceptable to term standards a planning mechanism and to describe the various types of standards that the industry is willing to supply, this characterization leaves out the other main player in the standards arena— the users. The providers need generalized standards, based on a reference model, that allow them to build the most generalized product

Figure 4-3. The model from the user's point of view

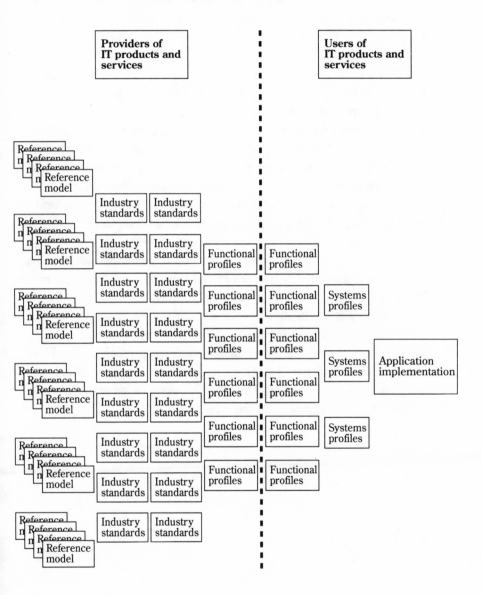

set possible while satisfying certain market needs. On the other hand, the users need answers to present or anticipated problems in their applications of IT products, specific either to themselves or to a class of similar users.

This chapter views standards as a marketing activity that tries to span the various levels of need in a chain of distribution of information. Standards are, after all, a method of codifying information. As the world becomes more complex and as more and more information becomes available, the crucial task will be to classify that information correctly so that it can serve a useful function: information overload is more dangerous than lack of information, since it eventually inhibits action. Right now, the IT standards arena is suffering from information overload. The five-stage model does not reduce the information in the system but it may make it more manageable.

If the thesis of this chapter is correct, it paves the way for an entirely new approach to standards and the standards process. Part 3 of this book looks at SDOs, ranging from the international organization through single-objective groups. None of these bodies has moved from the two-stage model, even though some of the single-cause groups are operating from the systems profiles arena. Until there is an awareness that there are various levels of standards, driven by user and provider needs, the practice of standards will continue to become more and more hectic.

PART II. STANDARDS

CREATION

5 . TOPICS AND METHODS

OF STANDARDIZATION

A little learning is a dang'rous thing;
Drink deep, or taste not the Pierian spring.

Essay on Criticism
Alexander Pope

This chapter looks at the practical discipline of standardization in terms of internal and external standards programs. The first section— on internal standards—focuses specifically on the engineering or design function of an IT company or corporation—the producer of the earlier chapters. The next section outlines the process of external standardization, again mainly from the practical point of view of the producers.

Internal standardization

Internal standardization is usually the creation of a process—based on either a new or an existing routine—to enhance the use of company resources. It is increasingly complex, increasingly difficult, and increasingly overlooked as a method of ensuring not only survival but also success in the current business environment. An internal standards program is one of the more difficult corporate functions to manage and make effective. In any company, numerous things can be standardized—from paperwork routines through personnel policies to design processes. Standardizing a process in these areas requires an understanding of the company, its management, its operating structures and strictures, and its culture. It must be done without compromising innovation yet must be implemented completely enough for it to offer some benefit. The standards writer and management must be competent—at least apparently—in both the process being standardized and the process of standardization in order to maintain credibility within the larger group.

Ultimately, the decision for or against standardization is based on the amount of resources required to provide a solution to a specific problem. Indeed, an internal standard can be viewed as an attempt to describe a method of using a scarce resource—usually labor—in such a way that it is utilized more effectively. Obviously, the perfect standard would allow resources to be used in the most effective fashion possible, but the determination of what constitutes this ideal depends on how a corporation views its resources. If a company prides itself on engineering and skilled labor is limited, then engineering will receive the brunt of attention. Similarly, a company that stresses its manufacturing expertise may use standards to strengthen its manufacturing processes. But if a standardized solution favors a particular resource at the expense of other, scarcer resources, its economic value is doubtful. The major effort in internal standardization must be to establish which resource is perceived as the most valuable to the company and then to determine if this resource is also the most scarce. If it is not, compromise—at the least—will be necessary to concentrate the standardization effort in the area that will produce the most benefit. Furthermore, there is the need to factor in organizational behavior—at times, the imposition of a standardized methodology may be completely counterproductive.

This leads to the question of *why* a company would or should standardize its internal procedures. In all cases, the answer should depend on whether or not there is a return from the standardization program, and the return can only be judged for the particular company culture. Because standards span an organization—from engineering design, through marketing (and sales), to manufacturing, and, finally, to field service—the application, as well as the method of application, varies and derives from varying culturally based moral precepts. Application of a standard in one company may spell success; application of the same standard in another company may spell disaster.

The next important question is who will enable the standards program within the organization. Without this enabling function, and the legitimization it brings, the entire standards effort is doomed.

A standards group should begin by determining what its own purpose will be. While this necessity is so obvious as to be axiomatic, it is neglected by many internal standards groups. If the standards group exists to codify repetitious and simple procedures, its focus and staffing needs will be different from those of a group attempting to standardize an esoteric technology so that it need be created only once. If the group's purpose is to free a scarce resource so that it can be used for more important things, this should be stated. If the group is going to standardize other aspects of the company to make the scarce resource more available, this, too, should be indicated. In effect, the group must identify how it plans to operate—and what its area of expertise is—and create a charter that can be used to inform interested groups, within and without the organization, of its intentions.

A major consideration, often overlooked, is that standardization may cross organizational or suborganizational lines. If a process in manufacturing requires input from accounting, the two departments may have different goals for the process. The standards group must recognize the potential conflict and mediate between the disparate needs so that agreement is reached on the underlying rationale and activities that support the process—and the standard. If the group creates a standard without this agreement, it will sabotage its own efforts, since the impacted groups may be forced to expend resources that are already in demand in order to repair the damage caused by the misguided standard.

With the decision to standardize made and the charter of the group established, the next step is to determine where the program should begin. Most standards departments are born of a company's need to ensure that its products are free of legal liabilities—that is, that they will not kill, maim, or injure someone or, in service companies, that they will not create or delete user systems and information. Meeting this aim may not determine where standards will help the most and which resource is the most valuable, but it does serve the very pragmatic purpose of protecting the company against liability lawsuits.

Ensuring that internal mechanisms conform to external expectations is probably as far as most companies go when they first institute a deliberate standards program. Other standards are added on an as-needed, as-written, or as-desired basis, usually very haphazardly. Because the planning range of many companies is so short (usually less than three years), internal standardization generally is an afterthought in the product development process, invoked only after the market requirements are listed, the product has been specified, and the design engineering cycle has begun. Yet, when standards are used in this way, it usually is too late to use effectively the benefits that standardization can provide. If a company has ignored a market need/ requirement in completing a product design, the product may not sell well. Retrofitting it normally requires a great deal of effort, as well as a great amount of frustration, and may be highly ineffective, since the product may have missed its window of opportunity in the market while it was being improved (fixed). Likewise, any need (internal or external) expressed by a standard should be stated explicitly prior to any major commitment.

The dictum "Do it right the first time," while trite, is very valid for standards. A standard is a planning tool, meant for use during conceptualization and to help eliminate the need for someone to redo, or to correct, or for some resource to be expended in reconstruction, rather than in creation. Unfortunately, there is no handy guide to when internal standards should be invoked: do so too early, and creativity is stifled; too late, and the product/process loses the benefit that prompted the standards to be created in the first place.

Deciding what to standardize is equally troublesome, because it can lead to acrimonious debates between the proponents and opponents of standardization. The dispute is over the border between legitimate innovation and frivolous reinvention. Take the wheel, for example, since it usually completes the cliché. Standardization proponents would argue that the correct implementation of a standards program would allow the creation of better chassis but keep the design of the wheel the same. Opponents of standardization would argue that, under this program, wheels still would be constructed of stone, which would limit the remainder of the design.

This problem is not resolved by choosing sides but by determining the purpose of the standardization program. In this illustration, the program should not disallow improvement of the wheel altogether; however, it should be focused on the concept of the wheel as the primary form of transportation—that is, it should disallow the creation of legs but encourage the development of pneumatic rolling devices. It is a matter of asking the correct question—one of the most challenging of all activities in business, not because of insoluble problems, but because of the difficulties of definition and understanding.

If decisions had to be made about only one standard, one product, one person, they would be reasonably easy. Usually, however, quite a few standards will be invoked at once; in some cases, they are contradictory, or their use may imperil other goals—such as profitability. The most dangerous plan that a company can follow is blindly to set a course and to move on that path, modeling a program after someone else's successes. The internal standards program must suit the corporate strategic plan. A standards program must be directed by an understanding of where the corporation is going, not by tactical considerations. And, if an organization decides that it needs a standard, it must remember that even blessed internal standards have limitations. Frank Feigin, a senior standards engineer at Digital Equipment Corporation, expressed it best when, in a fit of outrage, he informed an engineering group that ". . . no matter how well a standard was written, it could not contravene the basic laws of physics."

The next topic is how to standardize. There appear to be three distinct methods by which a company can bring about internal standardization. Usually, a firm will pursue variants of all three, depending on the company, program, time, and any of a host of other variables.

The first method is to use a regulatory style, which assumes that a standard can be written explicitly and definitively and usually will be mandatory. The regulatory style is most suited to a mature, evolved industry or to the portion of such an industry that is least susceptible to change. For matters that are regulatory in nature or that deal with product safety, the regulatory style is ideal. Additionally, this style may be used in manufacturing processes where quality programs mandate a single procedure in order to fabricate a product that must meet stringent quality standards, although it is necessary to ensure that the application of this type of standard does not quell helpful innovation.

Standards imposed by a regulatory style are especially liable to be used as substitutes for planning. Moreover, this style of internal standard enforcement soon causes any standard to become an end in itself. Forgetting why the standard was imposed in the first place, people begin to devote as much energy to getting around it as to following it, especially if the standards program merely legitimizes a poor decision or a forgotten requirement. This eventually will require the attention of a police force or a full-time enforcer. Since the primary goal of standards is to save resources, this method appears to be self-defeating—after all, bucking the standard should be permitted if it allows the organization to use resources more effectively. Nonetheless, the regulatory style sometimes is pursued with tremendous vigor, since it seems safe and allows people to fall back on rules in a pinch.

The second style can be described as laissez faire. In effect, it allows the developer to ignore or to omit the use of standards. There is a major difference between an existing standards program that is not utilized and a standards program that merely does not exist. Where there is no standards program, there is the possibility of developing a meaningful one. Where a standards program exists and is ignored, the program has no meaning and little chance of acquiring any. This situation, closely related to anarchy, can serve a viable function in an environment of reasonably narrow, noninterrelated product lines but is dangerous in the presence of interdependence. Software seems to be especially vulnerable to this type of style: multiple editors, multiple interfaces, and multiple instructions are the order of the day in this portion of the industry and eventually may spark user resentment, since the absence of commonality causes the users to expend resources in training that the use of a standards program would have saved.

The final style combines aspects of both the regulatory and laissez-faire methods. It is probably the most difficult to exercise, since it requires that every potential standard be evaluated for its return and impact on the company and customers. If standardizing a particular process, product, or activity is critical to the company's survival, the decision must be made to standardize and then to enforce that standard. If a standard is not especially necessary, then the decision must be made to unstandardize. Difficulties arise, of course, when there is a need for standardization and an equal need for innovation and speed. In these cases, standardization becomes very complex. Ultimately, however, management must make the decision actively, since default decisions have a way of setting unfortunate precedents that return to haunt the defaulter—or the defaulter's successor. It is on these occasions (which should be relatively rare, if the program is managed correctly) that the standards management of a company proves its worth.

A company can gain the most by standardizing on products, processes, and methods that require a great deal of expertise to create (such as an internal bus scheme or complex software, a manufacturing process, or a quality program). The company should focus on its strengths and reinforce them through the use of standards. The decision to proceed in this effort is the domain of the company management; it should not be left to chance and the internal standards man-

65

agement. It normally is, however, which is all the more unfortunate because these things are very hard to standardize.

Rather than take on the challenge of standardizing in complex areas, people often turn to things that should not be standardized at all, usually those processes that are the easiest to quantify and so adapt well to the quantifiable processes of standardization. Typically, these are ancillary processes that serve to enhance products, development processes that require the most flexibility and responses, or any process that can adjust to deal with an uncontrollable external or environmental influence. These processes are poor candidates for standardization since, by their very nature, they are either exceptions to a larger process or "one-time-special good deals."

It is equally dangerous for a manager to seek a proven solution to a difficult problem, instead of attempting to determine the problem's real nature. Often, a standard solution will be seized upon, based on historical precedence and safety or because it worked in the past; innovation and thinking are displaced by the safe, rule-based answer. Reliance on standards to solve difficult problems, not the presence of standards, stifles innovation and creativity. Correctly written, standards are applicable to many situations; they are not, however, a panacea. Blind adherence to standards—or the substitution of standards for the real understanding and solution of a problem—is the most serious blunder that an internal standards group can commit. In fact, it can be fatal to a company if it becomes endemic and prevents the adoption of new procedures or technology essential to survival. Obviously, the final responsibility for guarding against this type of error is management's, for it is management that sanctions the actions of the standards group in the first place. Again, this is where management is critical.

It is also where internal standards management should or must be made responsible for proposing valid areas for standardization to corporate or organization management. Each standard or proposed standard should be examined from the point of view of its impact across the board; if a single standard acts as a gate to a host of other activities or serves as the common thread, it had better be a very good standard. Unfortunately, it usually isn't.

Another error crops up when a standards group standardizes two similar but competing processes. This is fairly common if the standards department is poorly coordinated. It is easy, especially in any high-change, high-technology area, to lose sight of where all of the processes that need to be standardized are headed. Occasionally, apparently competing processes come to a common end. This sets the stage for some internal bickering and forces the standards department to retract one or both of the standards—again, very embarrassing.

A variation on this theme involves the refusal to standardize two or more processes that appear to have a common starting point, since it is intuitively obvious that they accomplish the same thing. If the hope is to standardize only one of the processes, it is necessary to ensure that they truly do accomplish the same thing in the same manner or that the processes are, in fact, the same. If they end at different points, they obviously are not the same, although one may be a valid subset of another. If they end at the same place, they may have used different processes to get there, in which case, an understanding of why the different processes were used is essential. In some instances, the processes are used for checks and balances; in others, they test reality at different points and so complement each other. And, of course, sometimes they do duplicate one another.

The standards group must carry out the planning and execution cycles responsibly, taking the time to review, revise, and even reject its proposals before passing them on to management. As a staff function, it should advise, not mandate, appropriate courses of action. Management must assume its share of responsibility and work to understand the validity of the proposals. And it is work: there are usually no criteria by which to judge these proposals because so little management theory covers the qualifiable aspects of standards as an aid to the planning and management function.

External standardization

External standardization covers standards activities outside the realm of the company. Where internal standards are relatively closed to anyone except the producer and the groups that the producer allows to participate, external standards suffer from no such constraints, and the full panoply of consensus standards become actively involved.

From a producer viewpoint, external standards are often a necessary evil. The best of all possible worlds for a producer would be to have a proprietary product, with no substitutions and no truly competing product available, in a market that was expanding as quickly as the producer could fill demand. The IT market, however, emphasizes change, technological innovation, and uneven market growth. All of these have combined to make standards necessary—to both the producers and the users.

The users have not taken as much advantage of standards as they could have, with the exception of the organized societies. The producers, however, must participate if they have any aspirations of leading the market. This is especially true now with the increasing numbers of value-added resellers (VARs) specializing in joining the systems of multiple vendors. Additionally, the explosive growth of all forms of computing—from personal computers to supercomputers—has made the closed, single-vendor shop nearly extinct. The user-mandated desire for interconnection has driven the collaborative efforts of the producers in the arena of standards.

The ability to participate in external standards is less a function of technical ability than it is of endurance. Because the United States tends to be focused somewhat on the short term, many people find the process too lengthy, too convoluted, and too cumbersome. The key to understanding and using external standards is to consider them as a strategic planning mechanism, one that is slightly more difficult to deal with than internal standards. If it is remembered that any external standard is an attempt to bring a bit of order to a chaotic market or to provide structure to an unstructured activity, the purpose of external standards becomes a little more clear. Finally, if the totality of the market is seen as a system, containing a great deal of momentum, a standard can be seen as an effort to direct that momentum. The larger the change, the greater the energy required. It is not a trivial task.

External standardization is a lengthy process. From the participant's point of view, it can be divided into two major areas—the preconceptualization stage, which takes one to five years, and the formal standards process, which can be broken down further into four main areas: conceptualization (up to a year), discussion (the same), writing (up to three years), and implementation (forever). The major activities under the control of the formal standards process—conceptualization, discussion, and writing—usually take between two and five years, depending on the amount of discussion and controversy that the proposal has generated. There is also a dependency on technology in this arena, which can stretch the cycle slightly.

Preconceptualization does not occur in any standards group at the present time. In effect, this is the stage where the market is examined to determine if there is a legitimate need for a standard. The need must exist—either in reality or in the market perception (which will act for reality). The idea for the standard must be applicable to the market in general, must be widespread enough to be accepted by a substantial clientele, and yet must be contained enough to be created or adapted/adopted. Ideally, a standard should "bring something to the table"—something that cannot be supplied by the existing standards/markets. If the need does not exist, because the market is not ready for the standard or for the concept, the originator may wish to try to drive the market in a correct direction, where "correct" is a relative term. It is here that fanaticism comes into play, since only someone with a mission will be willing to take on this thankless task.

Once the market need is determined or created, it must be examined to see if it can be met with a standard. This step may be patently obvious, but there is much room for abuse here. Occasionally, standards are created to satisfy a user's spurious need or want stemming from the limitations of current technology or a misunderstanding of the problem. In effect, a standard is being used to solve a nonstandard problem. It is the equivalent of using software to solve a hardware problem or using hardware to solve a software problem. In either case, a solution has been found—but is it appropriate for the actual problem or does it actually mask a larger, unseen problem? An example of such a solution would be the decision to increase an interface capability beyond the ability of a user to exploit it or to standardize a new interface without providing a substantial improvement over the current standard. Cosmetic proposals that seek to utilize standards to cover a design flaw or a marketing error also may appear to be valid at first glance but will prove false on deeper inspection.

The most common failing of the novice standards participant is to attempt to standardize items that should not be standardized—a technical architecture, for example. By definition, a standard is reasonably unchanging; therefore, the only time that an architecture should be standardized is when it is no longer subject to change—and when an architecture is no longer subject to change, it is dead. ("Architecture" here is meant to denote a particular family of computer systems; it is not meant to imply a global view of computing.) The skill of standardization for a producer lies in standardizing only enough of those things that the user needs to permit constancy in the user's operation. Anything that should and must change to take advantage of changes in technology or conceptualization and that remains hidden from general knowledge and access (and therefore usage) should not be standardized.

For the user, the skill in standardization consists of standardizing those things that should remain constant, while permitting innovation to continue. At the same time, the user must espouse standards that the producers are able and willing to implement. If a standard is technically correct and philosophically proper but impossible to implement for most of the major producers, then its success in the market will be limited. If the purpose of the process is to make a standard that is acceptable and available to a large part of the market, it is sometimes necessary to postulate a less-correct solution to ensure that this objective can be reached. As was noted earlier, a standard is a workaday solution to a problem and not the ultimate technical response.

The users shoulder a large responsibility. The implementation of a standardized solution usually costs the producer some resource, and the provider will pass those costs along to the ultimate user. Over time, the economies of scale—a larger user base, a greater understanding, more acceptance—may allow the provider either to maintain or to lower the cost of the item, but the user first must be willing to accept and pay for the new standard. At times, the price associated with the use of a standard is not insignificant; it requires discipline and the willingness to change procedures and adapt to a different and occasionally more complex method of goal achievement. Users that opt for a less-expensive nonstandard solution are sending a very clear signal that ultimately can cause a vendor to abandon a standards effort. If there is a discrepancy between what a consumer wants and what a consumer is willing to pay for, providers usually will provide what will sell, not necessarily what is correct.

When a real problem and a valid potential solution are found to exist simultaneously, the preconceptualization stage is nearly over. The only problem left is finding an appropriate standards association to initiate the solution. This effort, in and of itself, can be very difficult. The standards proposer will find either a plethora of potential standardization committees or will be unable to find any at all. In nearly all cases, it is best to start with the national forum; within the United States, this would be the American National Standards Institute (ANSI), which usually can direct a visionary toward a society or committee that can handle the problem. This can take some time, however—standardization is not an exercise for the impatient.

Once the proposal has been submitted to a standardization body, the initial phase of the formal standards process begins. Conceptualization is a recognized part of the standards process, although it is described only vaguely in many standards organizations' operating procedures. During this phase, the standards organization with jurisdiction over the program will review it for technical feasibility, with an eye to preventing the initiation of a standard requiring a major breakthrough in engineering for success. A standard, after all, is supposed to be something that can be used by the general public and not just a few practitioners of an esoteric art.

If the proposal is found to be technically feasible, it is reviewed for economic feasibility—justification of the need. This is usually no more than a symbolic review, although it may, in the future, become more and more significant as standards become increasingly interrelated.

After passing these reviews, the proposal is advertised in a standards bulletin or similar organ to attract individuals interested in participating in the standard's development. When enough participants have been found, the standard is assigned to an existing or a newly created committee, the officers of the committee are appointed, and the committee commences work.

In some cases, the standard never generates enough interest to permit the formation of a committee. It is then up to the sponsor (or the fanatic) to arouse the necessary industry interest or to withdraw the proposal. Trumpeting the proposal in the popular and trade press seems to work fairly effectively. Also effective, but requiring more effort, is gaining the interest of the government or of a legislator, who then provides free publicity. Finally, the originator can set about converting people to the cause individually. While this last approach takes much longer, it usually is the most effective; both the popular press and the trade press constantly are filled with standards ideas of varying validity, and legislators are fickle at times.

Assuming that the standard proposal has found a home, the committee begins by determining the scope and nature of the work facing it, gaining some idea of the impact of the standard on which it will be working, and estimating the kinds and amount of resources that it will need and the time that it will take to complete the process. With this rough information, the chairperson of the committee can initiate the discussion phase. Interestingly, this phase is mentioned in no description or operating procedure, and everyone usually roundly condemns it as a waste of time and resources. However, it is vitally necessary to the success of the consensus standards process.

First of all, the discussion phase allows the committee to decide exactly what is being standardized. It permits alternative technical and philosophical views to be worked out in a nonhostile, nonbinding environment. The exact definition of the scope of work for the standard can be considered, and the methods presented in the proposal for solving the problem can be reviewed. It is at this stage that the originator of the proposal ofttimes loses control of the standard. The originator usually has a specific solution and has found a problem for which that solution is applicable and so tends to be blind to alternatives. There is a potential for extreme divisiveness during this stage, and, with the nature of the problem that the committee is trying to solve always in mind, the chairperson must resort to much skill and cunning to ensure that the committee does not self-destruct.

As the committee decides exactly what the conceptual basis for the standard is, work also can proceed on the technical issues that the committee faces: the choice—usually—of the technology that will be employed; the sophistication that is necessary; the reliability of the components; and a host of other topics that must be considered before work on the standard can proceed with any degree of consistency. Again, it is up to the committee chair to make sure that these issues at least are placed before the members, not for a final decision, but just to make them aware of some of the decisions that they eventually will face.

During this stage, the parties who will be impacted by the standard have the right to join the committee and comment on the proposal. Users, providers, and the government use this period to lobby their needs into the standard. It makes for organized chaos in the committee but a chaos that is very productive. Interested parties have a chance to exchange views, perhaps giving each participant a wider understanding of the issues—an important step toward the consensus that is so vital in the later stages of the standards process. Additionally, the turbulent discussions spark an excitement that begins to notify the market that a standard is coming. Market acceptance of the standard begins with these discussions on the committee structure, concepts, and technical analysis. In effect, the discussion stage places a marker in the market, reserving a space for the future standard.

Finally, the committee reaches the phase of the standardization process with which everyone is familiar and in which the technical merits of many participants shine. Now the concept is crystallized and translated into reality—yet the transformation can be exceedingly boring.

The purpose of writing a standard is to turn ideas and concepts into repeatable, understandable, and concise language. Unfortunately, language is inherently imprecise, and, since some words gain their meaning from context, the potential for misinterpretation is great. A standard must be written as clearly as possible, with a very precise choice of words. Fuzzy, pejorative, and highly emotive words routinely are avoided. But no matter how carefully a standard has been composed, the original wording, however clear to the author, may be vague or confusing to the uninitiated reader—who, after all, is the standard's ultimate consumer.

The standards writers must guard against making implicit assumptions or using terms and language that only the experienced will understand. The language should allow only one interpretation. If the standard is meant to permit more than one implementation of this interpretation, this can be designed into the standard; however, it should be absolutely clear that only the implementations—not the interpretation—are several.

While the standard is being written, the review cycle required for consensus makes its presence felt. The drafts are reviewed by the committee and by all of the more general and senior standards organizations and subjected to revision. Comments are answered, more changes made, and the momentum begins to build. As this goes on, the standard begins to receive notice from the market. The marker placed in the earlier phases is getting ready to be called. When it is, technical expertise gives way to marketing know-how.

The first requirement is that users become aware that a standard is available. Normally, in the United States, this is the responsibility of the national standards body, which publishes and sells these standards. However, since a single IT standard rarely will be pushed by the national organization, which is responsible for standards from all industries, it is up to the specialized standards group to publicize the standard. In the United States, the Accredited Standards Committee for Information Processing Systems (ASC X3) is one of the primary channels through which new standards information is disseminated. Although this is not one of X3's official functions, its numerous committees, which work on nearly all major IT standards, provide a forum where members can meet to discuss standards activities. Because it is devoted exclusively to IT standards, X3 and its committees have a strong, focused interest and high expertise in this area, as compared to other organizations that participate in the standards process as a sideline. Additionally, the Computer and Business Equipment Manufacturers Association (CBEMA) is collocated with X3, which makes providing standards information to this industry lobbying group relatively convenient.

The primary method for disseminating standards information continues to be vendor/association campaigns. Vendors include information about standards in their advertising and product brochures, consultants sell consulting services that are predicated upon standards, and the industry goes out of its way to convince users that standardized products are superior.

There is no clear-cut method for standards implementation. The ultimate purpose of a standard is to make the market more efficient, to permit users to have a common metric, and to allow the sale of additional features above and beyond the standard. There should be a market pull for standards that indicates that users are aware of them, know how to demand them, and understand the implications of standardization. At present, the market pull for standards is very slight, frequently evident only in boilerplate procurement requests, stating "Must conform to all ANSI standards" or "Must meet all National Standards for I/O interfaces." It is in this area that much work remains to be done—and it is here that providers have the least leverage.

Conclusion

There is no clear conclusion to this chapter. It could go on indefinitely with cautions and warnings, tales from experience and case studies. The purpose of the chapter initially was to survey methodology and topics for standardization. However, I continue to believe very deeply that each program of standardization is unique to the group that wishes to standardize. Programs vary with organizational behavior, expectations, needs, perceptions, place, and time. If there are any constants, they are based on an organization being able to isolate the variables that it believes are essential to its success, to understand the nature of a standards program, and then to tie the variables to the program.

Standards are powerful tools and should receive the same degree of management interest as any other staff planning function; if they do not, they can turn quickly and cause more havoc than existed before their development. Much like Frankenstein's monster, a standards program may be initiated with good intentions but end up destroying its creator.

6 . THE ORGANIZATION AND

CONSENSUS STANDARDS: ISSUES

> Myself when young did eagerly frequent
> Doctor and Saint, and heard great Argument,
> About it and about; but evermore
> Came out by the same Door as in I went.
>
> *The Rubaiyat of Omar Khayyam*
> Edward Fitzgerald

There are no hard and fast rules for creating a standards group and placing it in an organizational structure. Beside having all of the problems of a normal organization, the standards group usually is suspect because of its strong external focus as an industry change agent. Furthermore, as with any market discipline, its actual contributions to a success are vague, although its relations to a failure often are explicit. Despite all this, however, as a change agent, the standards group must work through other organizational groups and needs the willing help of the organization to succeed. What follows is an overview of issues that should be considered when attempting to establish a program that will allow an organization to participate successfully in an external consensus standards program.

The business of standards

Why would a company, in the business of doing business, embrace standards? The arguments against the use of standards are, at times, overwhelming. If you have a truly unique solution, for example, why share it with competitors who don't have your abilities? And there is the argument that standards decrease a company's ability to innovate and to meet changing market requirements and, at times, even prevent change by increasing market inertia. On the other hand, if you are a fast follower, standards may hinder your ability to get to the market quickly with a follower product that has some added value. Finally, many claim that the intelligent provider will offer solutions as the market demands them, regardless of whether standards exist or not.

Complicating the equation even further is the fact that standards are not an all-or-nothing approach. A company can use standards in some areas, and reject them totally in others. A company producing a brilliant proprietary solution may, and usually does, demand from its suppliers parts that meet some form of standard, whether of quality, performance, or size. The company will use standardized metrics to test itself against the market. It will make use of standard formulas to avoid being preyed upon illegally by competitors. If it produces parts that have electrical components, it will meet certain test-house standards that ensure the safety of its products and will rely on the national electrical codes to see to it that its appliances are provided with adequate and correct power. The list can be continued to the point of distraction; the point is that all firms impose and expect to have available certain standards.

A more appropriate question, then, is: Which standards does a company/association/firm choose to uphold and which does it wish to avoid, and how are these decisions made? Logically, it is safe to assume that a firm will support standards that help it and will ignore or refuse to support standards that are irrelevant or inimical to its interests. This does not answer the question, however; it merely casts it in a different way. The answer, I believe, lies in the firm's perception of itself and the market in which it is involved.

A firm can be described as risk neutral, risk adverse, or risk seeking. Further, each aspect of the firm has its own risk-acceptance or risk-avoidance characteristics. The more a firm is risk adverse, the greater will be its reliance on regulations and standards as a possible hedge against risk and potential failure. A firm that is risk neutral will tend to view standards dispassionately, using them when and as necessary. Risk-taking firms will tend not to use standards, seeing them as limiting factors in their pursuit of business, although some firms are willing to accept a different risk by attempting to grow and then lead the market with a standardized product.

In the end, an organization can be seen as a collection of individuals and as a reflection of their ideas and activities. This seems to bring us back to where we started: individuals who believe in standards will use them, while individuals who don't, won't.

When Max Weber was trying to discover why rational capitalism was a distinctly Western phenomena, he came to the conclusion that a primary reason was the rational structure of law and administration. Without this rational structure, Weber reasoned, it would be impossible to predict, with any degree of certainty, the returns available to the investor capitalist. And without these calculations, there would be no incentive to engage in a rational capitalism.

Weber also observed that Western capitalism is influenced strongly by technology; for that matter, it is technology driven. A technology need not have originated in the West—consider, for example, algebra, the decimal, and other technological achievements that we have adopted from other cultures. What did originate in the West, however, was the application of various technologies as solutions to problems that appeared, at first, to have no connection to them.

Weber's comments on capitalism provide insight into why standards—especially voluntary consensus standards—function as well as they do. Fundamental to the definition of standards in Chapter 3 was a belief in the essential rationality of the market. The use of standards adds rationality to the market and provides yet another rational incentive for investment in it. Standards permit some quantification of the market prior to engaging it; that is, standards can give a perspective on the market, which, when joined with other indicators, can furnish a method of anticipating and measuring it. This added rationality may take several forms, serving to indicate a common acceptable path or, conversely, an absolutely unique and therefore extremely valuable solution or acting as a test/proving ground for a product concept. It is another tool for a rational manager to use.

When a firm claims to reject standards, it is in fact rejecting the use of standards in its marketing process. "We don't use standards" really means "We choose not to produce products according to what conventional market wisdom states that the market presently needs and will demand." This choice usually is predicated upon a firm's belief that it can provide a solution superior to that which the market has endorsed. While this approach may be justified, with the advent of standards that describe systems of products and services, changing the market with a proprietary solution is less and less viable, unless the solution is a quantum improvement over competing alternatives.

How to start a program

Too often, a standards program is initiated without regard for the consequences of this activity on both the standards participants and the organization with its multiple interdependencies. Yet planning and thinking of the long-term rationale and interplay that the group responsible for the program must have constitute a challenge that should never be avoided. It is easy to decide to whom and where a group should report; determining what will be done with the ideas that such a group exports (or imports) is a far more difficult task.

Once the rationale for the existence of a program is established and the responsibilities of the standards group have been considered, it is necessary to place the group in the organization. I would recommend placing the standardization function in a department that meets two basic criteria: it is sure enough of itself not to need the function but is capable of using the function to impose positive change on the larger organization. Standards are only guides; an organization must know how to use them if they are to serve any purpose. Because there are so many standards (and so many standards-developing organizations), a department that does not have a strong internal belief system and ability to make its own decisions will tend to be driven by standards rather than drive and use them. Such strength also will allow the department to accept and implement external ideas without feeling that its own competence is being threatened. (Both self-assurance and self-awareness are necessary, but, if a choice must be made, I believe that self-assurance is the more important of the two. Self-awareness can follow from self-assurance; the reverse usually is not true.) Of course, if the standardization function is placed in a self-assured, self-aware, but essentially powerless department, the impact of standards on the organization will be diminished substantially. The department that owns the function of standardization must be able to influence the business planning of the organization, since standards ultimately are an economic activity. Within the IT industry, the most common placements are in the engineering or in the marketing activities, depending on which function has the role of driving the organization's response to the external environment.

The next problem is deciding how to staff the standards group. Again, this is not a trivial task. The type of standards representative will depend on the rationale for the creation of the group. If the standards group is supposed to exert a major influence on the activities of the organization, then it should be composed of individuals who are viewed by the organization as having the necessary understanding and competence to effect that change. For example, if the locus of power in a company is the engineering function and standards will be used to impact the engineering cycle, then the engineers must be able to respect the standards delegates. The standards representatives also must have a talent for dealing with people, as well as being competent in their technical discipline, since they will be required to sell the goodness of the standards inward and the goodness of their organization outward. Finally, will the standardization group consist of a few professional standards people, who will matrix manage a large organization of standards volunteers, will it consist of a large centralized staff that alone has responsibility for standardization within the parent organization, or will it fall somewhere between these two extremes?

Deciding on the structure of the standardization group also can be interesting. If there is an accepted model for the group within the larger organization, there is no problem. If no such model exists, two factors largely will decide what the group's structure will be—the type and nature of the people involved and the type and nature of the function that the group is expected to accomplish. If the group contains brilliant iconoclasts, no structure will serve well or long, especially one that is highly centralized. However, if the standardization group is expected to impose its activities on the larger organization, a highly centralized organization probably would be most efficient. While I tend to believe that form follows function, in this case, it also must accommodate the idiosyncrasies of the people involved and the role that these people have in the larger organization. Finally, the interfaces that the group must have, should have, and may have should be specified. Knowing with whom to talk and when is a key ingredient in consensus standards.

While a manager who has time and discretion may be able to take advantage of these guidelines, what happens to the ordinary manager who suddenly is confronted with the need to participate in consensus standards activity? The usual approach is to graft the external group onto the internal group. Economical in terms of time, complexity, and people, this seems like an easy solution to a complex problem. Usually, it is completely disastrous. The two types of standards have only their name in common. Where the internal group tends toward enforcement and regulation, the external standards group must favor conciliation and consensus. One is charged with immediacy: the other with planning. The two groups have fundamentally different philosophies and operating constraints. If they are merged, they should be separated by some nearly impermeable membrane that will allow the flow of ideas but not of restrictions and problems. The operation only will work under the supervision of a reasonably competent manager and subordinates, who realize all of the complexities.

How the program should function

To begin, the larger organization must decide the nature of its involvement in external standards. While the standards-developing organizations (SDOs) encourage participation and minimize the cost to the delegates in their fee structure, the requisite travel and participation are expensive. Meetings vary in length and location—from one-day planning meetings in Washington, D.C., to three-week Plenaries in Sydney—and each delegate is responsible for paying her or his own way. Each organization must decide where and to what extent it wishes to participate. If an organization has an outstanding interest in a single field, it may choose to participate only on those committees directly related to that interest. It may escalate its involvement and become active either vertically (in the parent committee) or horizontally (in more standards committees). It may decide to become involved in the administrative arenas (nearly all of the administrative committees have open membership) or perhaps in the national organization. The depth and level of participation will depend on what the parent organization sees as the payback of the standards group and on how far it can support the group's activities.

The effectiveness of a standards delegate derives to some extent from the credibility of the sponsoring organization. If a delegate represents an organization that always has denigrated standards, the delegate will have a more difficult time than would someone representing an organization that has encouraged standards. The sins of the parent are visited upon the children—a delegate from a suspect organization likely will be credited with the same aspirations as the parent. Vacillation in participation can be seen as a lack of commitment, which can lead to disaster, since the level of respect—and the concomitant influence—that a delegate can expect in the committee will be based in large part on her or his competence and commitment. If the delegate's commitment is deemed lacking by association, the value of participation will decline.

This type of perceptual bias is never static, because the participants are engaged in a dynamic business, where alliances change with business and political considerations. Politics, whether positive, neutral, or negative, are never far from the surface. While the individual delegates are primarily responsible for these undercurrents, the company, the committee, the committee chair, the national body, or any of a dozen other influences can combine to create the political atmosphere in which both the committee and the delegates operate.

Once the producer understands the structure of the committees and the implications of their work, the problem arises of how to participate. There is the "observer" participant, who simply observes and reports to the company. (The use that the company will make of the report—ranging from filing it away to using it as the basis for the next product or system design—should have been decided at an earlier time.) There is the "participating" participant, who takes an active role in the proceedings, shares knowledge, and supports—or opposes—particular developments. And then there is the "contributing" participant, who advocates a solution or technology that has been contributed by her or his sponsoring organization or who badly wants a particular technology to be accepted to permit expansion of influence. (All of these observations apply to users as well; producers have no lock on the advocacy role in standards organizations.)

Once the delegate understands what the goal of the sponsoring organization is and how the committee helps or hinders that goal, the delegate begins to function as part of the committee and part of the standards process. The enabling process becomes important here. If participation is critical to the survival of the sponsoring organization (in either a positive or a negative sense), then the delegate must have the complete support of the sponsoring organization. If a delegate does not know where compromise is possible and where it is impractical, then she or he already is crippled, and participation can turn into a fiasco. Also, if a delegate does not understand the consensus standards process or the parliamentary procedure of the process, then the potential for success becomes even less.

Another benefit of enabling the delegate is that he or she can funnel quantities of information back into the sponsoring organization: competitive information (the positions that other organizations took), technical information (what the industry seems to believe is the correct technical way to proceed); marketing information (what the committee, composed of industry representatives, believes will occur in x years). In other words, the standards delegate can provide much more than technical information and positions, if she or he knows that the organization wants or needs it. Conversely, if there is no clear enabling mechanism or if the standards process is not understood clearly, the delegate will not be able to contribute nearly as much.

Obviously, enabling the delegate within the sponsoring organization is critical. Because the delegates to standards meetings are all volunteers, there is no formal structure to ensure that the committee work will proceed in any particular fashion. If the delegates know why they are attending and each hopes to gain a benefit for the sponsor, there is some motivation to move the process along. If the delegate is not sure of the sponsor's reasons for participation, the motivation becomes questionable, and the direction fuzzy; moreover, the delegate unknowingly may approve of a committee action counter to the sponsor's interests.

How to fund the program

Funding should be tied to the concept of return. A modified zero-base budgeting concept can be applied—what would happen if an organization chose not to participate in the standards process? In many cases, nothing would happen. Most IT companies are well served by standards and adhere to them when they need to or must. Lack of active participation is acceptable if a company does not need standards (because it produces a unique nonstandard product) or if it is a follower in a standardized area. Lack of participation, however, means that an organization cannot impact the process and must, therefore, follow it willy-nilly.

After an organization begins to participate, each increase in involvement should be analyzed in terms of what the organization will gain from the participation and what it would lose if it did not participate. At times, participation may only confirm a worst suspicion, but such confirmation can be valuable. On the other hand, if there is no participation, the organization may miss a potential opportunity to influence a standard in a way that will make the market served by the standard more friendly. This analysis is difficult—lost-opportunity cost is highly subjective, especially in standards, where the outcome is never certain. (Participation in the national administrative committees and organizations is the most difficult to justify: the national organization is supposed to serve the interests of the industry as a whole; the organization must be convinced that the national programs—and the entire standardization effort—are necessary to the future of the industry to commit to this level of activity.) In many cases, a manager can make the analysis and then justify the choice only after the fact. However, the rationale and evaluation are important, since they provide the metric by which the success of the standards group can be judged and future actions taken.

One of the chief characteristics of standards in commercial industry is that they can be seen as an enabling activity by an organization about to undertake something. In the past, producers often overlooked this function of standards, either from lack of knowledge or lack of need, while users ignored it because they preferred to deal directly with the producers, rather than with the industry as a whole. Now, more and more providers recognize how standards enable an enterprise to begin, forming part of the functional (market) plan—a proactive process used to permit a product to come into being. The users see standards as a prerequisite at times and consider them to be an incremental, but positive, activity. By contrast, the governmental use of standards seems to be devoted more to cost constraint or cost lessening. Lack of standards, in a governmental environment, is a disabling activity.

In the end, however, money must come from somewhere to do something. The something that standards do is dependent on the organization's structure and belief in the role that it wants to play. The somewhere that the money comes from, however, should depend on one major consideration—who benefits from the activity of the standards group? If marketing is receiving all of the benefit but engineering is footing the bill, the standards effort is highly unlikely to survive a budget crunch. While requiring those who benefit to pay seems obvious, it is not a one-time exercise; it is advisable, every now and then, to check who is helping to pay the bill and whether they are getting results equal to or greater than the amount that they are contributing.

Standards as a discipline

Considering the practice of standards as a discipline in its own right will be difficult for many people who think of standards as an extension of regulations, where the main responsibility of the participant is to understand the technology of her/his industry well enough to be able to explain it to people who are considering regulating it and to elucidate why things are done the way that they are without using the phrase "We've always done it that way." This point of view is common among participants in today's standards activities within the information technology industry, in which the criteria for participation often seem to be limited to extreme technical competence and the ability to be a persuasive advocate for a particular technical solution.

Certainly, standards is a very technical discipline that requires great expertise in the area under consideration. Because the use of standards seems to be concentrated in disciplines that are more technically driven (that is, more capable of being described in precise metrics with established interrelations), there will continue to be a demand for highly competent technical people to formulate and write the standards. The emphasis will change slightly from a product to a systems orientation, and the technical expertise demanded may be used to describe future systems instead of present products, but the necessary talent will continue to be the ability to translate abstract technologies into written descriptions that are applicable and useful in a technical and business arena.

With this need firmly established, a new participant, the "technical engineering/business manager," slowly will be brought into the standards arena. This somewhat awkward title reflects the bundle of attributes with which the participant must be endowed. In effect, this person must understand both the technical and business needs of the particular company or group represented, the purpose of the proposed standard and its relations to other existing and proposed standards, the methodology of the consensus standards process, and the needs of the standards committee and possess the ability to plan and coordinate all of these simultaneously and to reframe problems and unruffle feathers, as needed. The term "business," as it is used here, refers to all of business, not merely the financial aspects. This concept—in which the organization rather than the balance sheet is central—is essential to standardization and the activities of the standardization process.

These technical engineering/business managers, representing the best that the industry has to offer, will become the actual managers of the standards process within the standards communities, serving primarily to practice what I refer to as "intersectional management." Intersectional managers do not manage in the traditional sense of the word; rather, they manage the potential areas of conflict—the intersections between the various competing individuals, factions, groups, segments, and theories—to ensure that conflict does not occur or that, if it does, its impact on the process is minimal. In addition, the various groups must be managed to move them toward and then to achieve a goal. Finally, the goal itself must be managed, since it may change with changes in the environment.

The intersectional manager is vitally necessary to the long-term success of the consensus standards effort. But one of the prerequisites for this style of management is competence on the part of the members of the committees. Such competence is assured only if the industry or the significant players are convinced that the consensus standards process is valuable and are committed to making it work.

7 . THE STANDARDS
ORGANIZATION

No man is an island, entire of itself;
Every man is a piece of the Continent.

Devotions Upon Emergent Occasions
John Donne

"A standards organization serves to create standards."

This widely accepted statement embodies the folk wisdom about standards; it is also false. It is just much easier to believe that standards are created and given to the industry than to believe that a portion of the industry helped (or could have helped) in their creation. Mysterious benefactors (and malefactors) have always fascinated people.

A more correct statement would be: standards organizations cause voluntary consensus standards to come into being. They are not, themselves, the creators of standards. Indeed, in most cases, their charters strictly prohibit them from writing standards; the most that they can hope to do is to provide a forum for the proper creation of standards. Because the standards organizations usually are recognized as representing more than one segment of an industry (users, providers, or interested parties), there is always some question about what constitutes "proper." The industry as a whole may appear to know where things are going, but each segment of the industry usually has its own opinion. The standards organizations were created to meld these divergent points of view.

Functions of a standards organization

A standards organization usually can be broken down into two components (in the simplest examination). The largest component is a standards organization's volunteer committees, consisting of representatives of the discipline served, which meet on a regular basis and actually write the standards that are published under the auspices of the standards organization. The standards organizations are the keepers of the management process and the rules for the committees. These committees (also called working groups and technical committees) have their own hierarchies, and each major committee may have subgroups reporting to it, some of which do the actual technical work assigned to the committee.

The second part of the standards group is the administrative section. While constant acts of administration occur in each and every committee, subcommittee, working group, and technical committee, there is usually only one centralized, professional administrative function for an industry-specific standards organization. This function usually falls under the purview of a group known as the Secretariat (the term has remarkably consistent usage across all standards organizations), which acts as the nonvolunteer portion of the standards group and is charged with ensuring the survival of the entire standards effort for the organization.

More specifically, the Secretariat monitors the initiation of work by the subsidiary committees and sees that schedules are met, that the proper work is being done, that the rules of development are followed, that rules for representation on the committees are equitable, that no prejudice is shown to any class or group, that the various members have adequate and sufficient access to the decision process, and that consensus is reached in the process. Some Secretariats also are charged with publishing the standards that are created, making sure that the standards are available (for a moderate fee) to anyone who wants them, keeping track of the myriad standards that are published, and causing them to be updated on an as-needed or regular basis (or deleting them). And, finally, through liaison, some Secretariats also keep track of what is happening in other standards organizations throughout the world, to ensure that there is a minimal duplication of effort.

If these were the only functions of standards organizations, it would be relatively simple to categorize them. Information technology standards organizations, telephony standards organizations, ferro-concrete standards organizations, and so on could be grouped into nice, neat, and discrete packages. However, life, people, and organizations being what they are, there are a multiplicity of standards organizations for each discipline.

For example, each major country has special requirements or expectations that mirror the needs of that country. Whether these needs are rooted in the national ethic, the national economic welfare, or simply a desire to be different is immaterial. At times, the country will use a standards organization to justify the setting of these requirements.

The use of a standard as a method of national control is contrary to the concept of voluntary consensus standards and falls into the category of regulation. If consensus standards are a true expression of market will and direction, the country that imposes artificial standards will find itself in one of two situations: either it will force the market to change according to its will (if it has economic importance to the market), or it increasingly will find itself isolated from the mainstream of products within the market and generally unable to share in the benefits that consensus standards provide, including technology transfer. In the long run, if it is true that standards are market driven, this situation will correct itself, and the inappropriate standards gradually will disappear as the market finds ways to circumvent them. In the short term, however, technical and economic disruption may occur, either in the industry or throughout the country.

When a country realizes that it does not have sufficient economic clout to force its concepts of standards on the market, it may choose to join a regional organization. The same conditions apply to this group as did to the country group, except that now the power of the region is behind the standards organization. If there is sufficient economic presence to force the market to accept the hoped-for change, the standards group succeeds.

Unlike the country organization, a regional group must compromise some of its members' interests over the longer run in order to preserve the whole. The question is, which country will sacrifice—or at least modify—national interests for the good of the larger group? The answer depends on where the national entity feels that it can find the greatest good.

Standards groups are not limited to country organizations, however. Although consensus standards groups are legitimized by their national organizations, sometimes many groups may represent the same discipline. This phenomenon occurs during the high-growth phase of an industry's life, when the discipline is expanding rapidly and new knowledge always is being created. The creation of this new knowledge causes even more expansion, which in turn causes the formation of new expert groups. As the expansion slows, the separate disciplines continue to grow, since growth is all that they know, and increased interaction (also know as turf wars) may result. Ultimately, the groups will begin to merge, until they become very much like one another, divided only by artificially assigned jurisdictional boundaries.

These boundaries continue to be valid only as long as they are accepted by the members of the groups. If a group feels that its survival is at stake, it may attempt to expand its jurisdiction, either by taking on a new technology or by seizing an extant technology and giving it a new nomenclature and set of attributes that fall under its charter. On the other hand, an established group, already loaded with responsibilities, may consider a new technology a mere duplication of what already exists. If some other body is willing to take the new technology under its wing and nurture it, this often results in the default creation of a new expert group. If the new technology succeeds, this expert group becomes the authority and can apply for acceptance as a standards group. Eventually, of course, two previously separate groups may end up doing the same activity with different technologies. It is at this point that the potential for conflict and destructive behavior becomes high, especially now that systems standards and applications standards (solution based) are replacing product standards (technology based).

In all of the above cases, the function of the standards organization is to represent the particular needs of their users. Standards organizations are composed of like-minded people who see these organizations as instruments that use their collective economic power to change and influence the direction of the market—something that individuals cannot do. This purpose of the standards organization often has been ignored, but it is central to understanding them. In some cases, the clients have a multiplicity of needs that the organization must fill, while in others, the groups focus sharply on a single need and market requirement, but all have a clientele to whom they provide a collective voice. The success and longevity of the standards organization is in direct proportion to its ability to convince its members that it has the power and ability to move the market in a direction that the members feel is correct.

One recent development in the high-technology arena is the growing lack of differentiation between technologies and, therefore, between clients. IT is becoming very similar to telephony in some of its applications. The users of standards are identifying the base technology with the application technology, and this lack of discrimination on the part of the users—understandable, given the change in the nature of standards—is beginning to complicate the lives of standards organizations tremendously. The client bases are no longer discrete. As the systems standards become more prevalent, the interrelationships among standards organizations will become more complex, and the management of the Secretariat, key to any standards organization, will become increasingly difficult.

The administration of a standards organization

Henri Fayol, a French managerial theorist at the turn of the century, ascribed the functions of planning, controlling, organizing, coordinating, and commanding to administration. I feel that this list, which I've ordered according to the importance of each function to the standards community, accurately describes the duties that the standards organizations' administrative groups should attempt to fill, although many of them, unfortunately, do not succeed in doing so.

Of all of the administrative functions, planning (Fayol's term was *prévoyance*, a word that emphasizes the forward-looking and strategic nature of the planning function) probably is the most important; at the same time, it is the most difficult. This difficulty derives from the nature of the administrative group; it cannot demand action from the members, since these members are all volunteers, joined by a common belief in standards and the standards process. Moreover, the Secretariat is nearly a pure staff organization; it has no line authority, except in the interpretation of the rules—and, even here, it is always open to challenge by members of the committees as well as by senior national and international committees. As a result, the Secretariats rely upon the members to accomplish the strategic planning function, which usually is delegated to a group that reviews and approves standards proposals. This group, because it is composed of members of the industry (producers, users, and general-interest groups), is a bit more able to impose its will; even so, all of its decisions are subject to an open and complete review at any time.

In any environment where there is no strong or congruent belief about the future, there is a difficulty with planning. For standards organizations, not only are there disparate views about the future, but each member has an interest in guaranteeing that his or her view of the future is actualized. In many instances, the planning function of the Secretariat consists of ensuring that the organization's perception of the future is broad enough to include the needs of all of the members while not penalizing the industry.

For Fayol, control was the aspect of administration that was concerned with ensuring that the other administrative functions were observed and carried out and that rules were followed. Because of the strict demands of the consensus approach to standards setting, distinct rules for ensuring consensus have evolved over time. Most Secretariats of standards organizations are very good at making sure that these rules are followed—a time-consuming and thankless job.

It is in this area that the administrators receive the most praise and condemnation. The rules, while important, often appear to be petty and pointless, more aimed at satisfying a bureaucratic requirement than at doing real standards work, yet they validate the entire process and assure that consensus standards are produced. At the same time, however, they should not be the ends in and of themselves. Their ultimate purpose is to produce in a fair and timely manner standards that meets market needs and requirements. If the rules inhibit this activity, then they, and their enforcement or interpretation by the administrators, have become counterproductive. There is a fine line between anarchy and totalitarianism in the standards world.

Organizing generally is part of the charter of the standards committee. Each committee organizes itself in a fashion that appears best to accomplish its perceived role and that mirrors the beliefs and desires of its members. While the senior standards organizations may provide general rules for membership, voting, and other functions, the independence of each committee in interpreting these rules is substantial.

There is a managerial concept that says that organizational form should mirror the strategy/belief of the organization. This concept is very important to standards committees that exist in a dynamic environment. If the organization or structure of such a committee is rigid and devoted to a singular end, the committee very well may become obsolete as the environment changes around it, since it will be tied into an organizational form ideal for activity that is no longer valid. The administrative function here is to ensure that the organizational aspects of the group are flexible and that there is a continuing inflow of members who can help the organization adapt to the changes in the environment. Again, the skill with which this administrative function is carried out is a major determinant in the success of the standards committee.

Coordinating is concerned with maintaining harmony in the organization and with keeping the organization moving toward its goals. It is not an unusual or especially difficult activity in a company or in most other enterprises. However, the Secretariat must coordinate the activities of a group of volunteers who have separate agendas, concepts, needs, and goals. It also must coordinate the needs of the specific standards committee with the activities of other standards committees in different areas. Again, the problem lies in accomplishing this coordination without the actual or implicit power to do so. And, again, the personnel of the Secretariat must keep everyone satisfied—or at least not too irritated—while pursuing a set of goals and objectives that reflect the wishes of the committee, which are also fuzzy. The role of the committee administrators is not so much to perform this function themselves as it is to encourage the members to do so. It requires patience, tact, and understanding, as well as a ruthless determination.

Finally, we come to the concept of command, best described as leadership ability and quality. The other functions need to be actuated by the Secretariat; all need to be done. Command is that intangible, unteachable ability to succeed in the management environment. It causes the other functions to be carried out; how well they are carried out depends on command. However, the metrics for predicting success are not clear; success usually is attributed after the completion of an arduous task or over the passage of time. *If* standards are produced that mirror what the industry wants and needs, *and if* they are produced in a timely manner, *and if* there is little contention in the organization, *and if* there is a willingness to undertake new challenges, *and if*. . . . Success is a judgment call and can be applied only in retrospect.

The burden of these five functions is tremendous, since the administration must manage them with little or no real power and authority but a great deal of responsibility. It is accountable to a host of people for all of its activities and operates in a spotlight. While a poor administration function will not paralyze the working groups or standards committees by any particular action, a good administration is essential to the continued success of the standards organization, since it provides continuity and serves as the organizational glue by keeping volunteers informed and interested and participating. Without this interest on the part of the volunteers, there are no consensus standards.

The working groups

The working groups—or technical committees, task groups, subcommittees, and so forth—are composed of volunteers representing all facets of the affected industry—the providers, the users, government, academia, interested or involved groups, and individual experts. It is in the working groups that the industry reaches consensus, that technical details are debated and resolved, and that actual standards are created.

There are usually no requirements involved in being a part of the standards process, other than having an interest in the standard under consideration and a desire to participate in its development. Membership dues are imposed, but these dues are intended to pay the administrative costs of the committee, not to impose an economic barrier—in fact, they can be waived by the committee if they are legitimately onerous and prevent participation. In general, however, all expenses associated with standards creation—from the mailing costs (usually assumed by the working group chair or secretary) to the payment of dues—are the responsibility of each individual.

Most organizations impose strict requirements for attendance at working group meetings. However, because the working groups meet relatively infrequently, attendance is one of the more observed points of etiquette. Each working group establishes its own administration (usually a chairperson, assistant chair, and secretary), decides its own meeting schedules and locations, and defines its own task within the charter that the standards committee has granted it, as well as within its area of expertise. Once this definition of intent is resolved, the group can put together its organization, set a proposed timetable, and begin its deliberations to complete the standard. To ensure fairness, there are fundamental rules intended to maintain equity in the structure.

A working group's deliberations should be relatively simple, since everyone is like-minded and working for the common good. Unfortunately, as I have pointed out before, the term "common good" not only is unclear at best, it is virtually meaningless in this context. When a working group begins its creative function, there is no guarantee as to what will emerge from the standards process—the common good is a complete unknown. It is the process of consensus—the interaction among members, the compromises and confrontations, and the ability to reframe questions so that they admit of a common answer—that leads the successful standards working group to its goal.

When a standard is completed, accepted, and implemented, a working group either can dissolve, or it can press on and take up the next challenge in its area of expertise. Its membership can change from meeting to meeting, or it can remain stable with a constant membership. Everything depends on the nature of the beast, and the beast is protean.

Conclusion

This chapter has tried to throw some light on exactly what a standards organization does, or is supposed to do, from an organizational perspective. This is not to say that all standards organizations function as described. I based my discussion on the American National Standards Institute model of consensus procedures; other national models reflect the predisposition within their own environments. All, however, function somewhat similarly. The structure may vary (within certain constraints), but the essential task of each standards group is to create standards that are viable, both economically and technically, consensus driven, and acceptable to its constituents. This last goal often is overlooked, yet being an assemblage of like-minded people imposes a certain bias even before a standard is created. However, this bias offers an advantage—the standard, when created, will mirror the needs and desires of the industry segment that it serves and probably will not lead its clientele down a costly and destructive dead end.

Imagine the whole, then execute the parts—
Fancy the fabric
Quite, ere you build, ere steel strike fire from quartz,
Ere mortar dab brick!
A Grammarian's Funeral Shortly After the Revival
of Learning in Europe
Robert Browning

This chapter will look at the mechanics of consensus standards creation in the United States. In some cases, it will employ the exact terminology of the American National Standards Institute; in others, the discussion will be flavored with my impressions and views and may not mirror precisely the intent of the ANSI language.

Methods of standards creation

While many other countries have a single organization dedicated to the creation of standards, the United States—under ANSI procedures—has three types of organizations that can create a standard: the Accredited Sponsor using the canvass method, the Accredited Organization (AO) method, and the Accredited Standards Committee (ASC) method. Each of these methods has its proponents and detractors. An examination of each will clarify the reasons for their creation. Much of the rationale derives from the culture of the United States and the essentially individualistic, competitive nature of business.

Accredited Sponsor using the canvass method

The Accredited Sponsor method of standardization is based on the idea that a given organization has an interest in seeing the creation of a particular standard, which has an interest group larger than the organization's constituency. The organization, which must be an approved (or at least a recognized) entity, thus sponsors a drive for standardization and begins the canvass method by inviting comments on the standard that it is proposing from anyone who cares or may be materially affected by it. The assumption is that a consensus on the proposed standard is extant; what is being sought is a confirmation of this consensus from the impacted parties and a demonstration of honest interest and intent in the standard. When the due process has been completed—and the due-process provisions apply to this and all other methods that produce standards—the standard is submitted for approval and eventual publication as a standard developed under the auspices of ANSI.

The benefits of the method are substantial. It moves relatively quickly (as the standard's world goes), it identifies the working and concerned parties interested in the arena, and it provides the community a chance to coalesce and help itself. However, the canvass method is appropriate only when substantial agreement on the thing to be standardized already exists. If there are multiple opinions on the need, solution, methodology, concept, and rationale for a standard, this method breaks down very quickly, becoming largely ineffective. Thus, the canvass method has been effective in the creation of non-contentious software standards, such as ADA. (There was contention about ADA as ADA but not about ADA as a standard.) It would not be successful in areas similar to the COBOL revision, which was marked by substantial divergence of opinion and numerous comments on the content of the standard.

In effect, participants in the canvass method can be compared to a group of people who assemble for a party. They share a common purpose and a certain familiarity with the activities expected, and, when the party is over, everyone goes home feeling satisfied. The intent is not to form a new concept but to reaffirm commonality and friendship.

The Accredited Organization method

In the Accredited Organization (AO) method, an already existent group completes a standard in an area in which it has direct and material interest amd a perceived expertise. Usually an industry trade group or association of industry experts or participants, the AO often has extant standards that are based on the methodologies of its profession or discipline.

The AO method begins with an Accredited Organization indicating to ANSI that it wishes to become certified as a standards-creating/writing body. To receive such certification, the AO must demonstrate its competence in the area of interest and its willingness to use an ANSI-approved consensus methodology to create standards. While these criteria do not appear to be burdensome, they can become a major point of contention. The consensus approach encourages anyone with a direct or materially affected interest to participate in the process of standards creation. If the organization is a professional society or a trade group, it must accept participation by those whose perception of the discipline is liable to be different from that of most members. In many AOs, the development of standards may have proceeded much more smoothly prior to the acceptance of the consensus approach. Once accredited by ANSI, however, an AO can produce standards that become American National Standards.

There are two major questions in this method of standards formation. The first is whether the group really possesses the necessary expertise. The second problem, more difficult to resolve, is establishing whether the group is operating in the best interests of the industry as a whole or merely attempting to maintain or increase its influence and power base. This extremely sensitive issue is addressed in part by the checks and balances of the standards system. It is assumed that, because of the honesty of the majority of the membership, an attempt to create a standard that precludes another's interest will not succeed. I believe that this usually will be the case; in this age, the specter of the evil conspiracy tends to be raised by interest groups trying to account for their inability to gain special treatment. However, the potential use of standards to protect the status quo is a constant worry with which the AO standards-development group must live. There is a great temptation to standardize only upon things that are familiar to the majority of the members—who, in the main, share similar educational and philosophical backgrounds. Ideas that come from outside the circle of expertise can be looked at with jaundice.

In general, however, the AO usually produces standards that have merit for the industry. This is especially true for the more mature, stable industries, where the knowledge is shared and is reasonably static. In more fluid environments, the ability of an AO to accommodate change while continuing to create meaningful standards is likely to become somewhat diluted.

The AO method is more complex than the canvass method. However, AOs accept this complexity because they generally exist for some purpose other than writing standards. Standards are a sideline. Usually, the exchange of professional ideas, industry knowledge, and shared experience is the ultimate goal of the AO.

To continue the analogy of the previous section, an AO's standards-creating group is comparable to a company bowling team. The bowling team is an offshoot of the commonality of the workplace. Without that underlying bond, the team probably would not have formed; if the team is dissolved, the commonality of shared work experience will remain. It is similar with the AO: without standards, the commonality of the shared professional discipline would remain; without the shared discipline—or professional society—standards would not be sufficient to hold the group together.

Accredited Standards Committee method

The Accredited Standards Committee (ASC) is formed for the specific purpose of creating standards in a contentious environment. It is, like today's corporation, a fictional creation that exists because it has to, not because it makes any real sense. The most sophisticated—and most contradictory—form of standards organization, the ASC takes groups and factions with diverse, even antagonistic, viewpoints and melds them into a semi-cohesive whole, with the aim of engineering a solution that encompasses all of the diversity while maintaining the benefits of individuality.

The key to the ASC is the Secretariat, held by a sponsoring organization, which provides legal, administrative, and financial backing for it. The Secretariat functions as the point of contact for ANSI and acts as the ASC's collective memory, as well as managing its administrative details. Without the Secretariats, the ASCs would become bogged down in administrative nightmares, and ANSI would be unable to cope with the multitude of contending committees.

The ASC usually has a committee structure—and an existence in which control and anarchy are kept in precarious balance. The creation of standards takes place in the committees; the administration of the committees (with concomitant rules) is the responsibility of their officers, who must observe the doctrine of consensus while maintaining their professional ethics and judgment. Generally, each committee is accountable to its senior committee, and the senior ASC officer (usually a chairperson) is responsible to ANSI, through the Secretariat.

The ASC normally decides how it wants to operate, what its charter encompasses, and (within reasonable limits) what its area of expertise is. It also decides how to structure itself to complete the necessary standards that lie within the scope of its charter and expertise, which should match. In effect, the ASC is the ultimate master of its own expectations, capabilities, and direction.

The areas to be standardized are publicized, and a call goes out for volunteers to staff the committees. When the committees are assembled, the development of standards begins. During the actual work, consensus is observed, and all those who wish to participate are heard. When the committee finishes its work, it creates a draft standard, which is forwarded to the Secretariat for action. The remainder of the consensus process is invoked, and, ultimately, a standard results.

The strength of an ASC standard is that it is the work of a cross-section of all interested parties. One of the main activities of the Secretariat is to ensure that no one group holds an overwhelming edge that might influence adversely the fairness of the standards produced. In theory, the standards are egalitarian, composed to favor all participants. However, I believe that it was Voltaire who pointed out that the laws of France were applied equally, forbidding both the rich and the poor from sleeping under bridges. A similar observation can be made about the ASC process—and here lies its chief flaw. Standards work is time-consuming and, hence, expensive in terms of that human resource. Additionally, it costs money to travel to standards meetings and to participate in the formal and informal dialogue that shapes standards. So, while the ASC process is open to both the rich and the poor, the rich have easier access to it. And, while the standards process is not as onerous as sleeping under bridges, being rich does make it less grueling.

Checks and balances

Central to an effective system of checks and balances is an understanding of the ultimate object for which one is attempting to gain equality and balance. If the purpose is to ensure that all parties have an opportunity to be heard, to comment, and to see the results of their comment and criticism, there usually is little problem. One designs a system in which every action is open to scrutiny, review, reaction, and contradiction. These characteristics usually are attributed to anarchy, yet they come reasonably close to defining the checks-and-balances system in the consensus standards process. This checks-and-balances system is predicated upon two major assumptions—that more than one person or group share a desire to standardize something and that their concern will translate into action. If these two assumptions are valid, the design of the system can be accomplished with a minimum of effort. If they are not valid, the system cannot possibly work.

The initial premise of the consensus process is openness. All activities concerned with the standard are open to public participation and comment. Rules for participation are available to anyone who cares to participate. The standard does not become final until all comments and objections are answered fairly and objectively within the process. Finally, because the process is voluntary, users, manufacturers, and the industry as a whole are not required to use the standard.

The secondary premise is that the standards developers understand that they are participating in an activity that may transcend individual or corporate needs and goals. If the participants are involved only to espouse their own causes, at the expense of the common good, the system will not work. Usually, however, a single individual or corporation does not make the move to increase the common good; rather, there is a sense that movement must occur, and, when a leader appears and asks if a new consensus can be achieved, this focuses the group momentum to produce a shift. Whether catalyzed by informal discussion, conversations, common sense, or a feeling of desperation, the shift takes place, prompted by the need to gain consensus, to achieve something that can be used by everyone. After all, this is the purpose of a standard.

In addition, standards groups usually are structured to strike a balance between the standards process matters—achievement of consensus, equality, and fairness—and the technical content of the standard—usability, completeness, and applicability. Generally, the organization that validates process is different from the organization that validates technical content. This ensures that the need for technical implementation and validity does not interfere with the larger need for consensus. If the standard is valid but does not represent consensus, it is not really a standard but, instead, an imposition of a solution. More commonly, the technical solution is correct, and the technical validation is intended to verify that the committee answered the question that was asked of it. This review, however unusual, frequently provides interesting, and occasionally dismaying, insight to the developers.

The standard is subject to appeal and review at all stages of development. Reviews are the responsibility of panels that become increasingly more process oriented and less technically oriented as the work proceeds. Initially, a review examines a proposal for technical merit. If the proposal is challenged and the challenge rejected, the protester has the right to appeal. At each stage of appeal, the appellant has the right to increase the level of review, until the claim reaches some form of ultimate appeals board. If a valid case for violated process is made at this level, the standard will be rejected and reworked. If the process is found to have been followed correctly, the proposed standard will be made an official standard.

The success of the entire process hinges on the existence of committed participants. If concern is lacking in the industry, the process may produce some interesting standards, but these may or may not be valid. The ultimate check and balance is an enlightened industry self-interest. The industry cannot afford to ignore the process; the greater its involvement, the more useful the checks-and-balances system. Apathy, not conspiracy, is most to be feared.

Time requirements and expectations

The time required for the creation of a standard is in direct proportion to the interest that the standard has created in the industry. Creation time also is directly proportional to the number of delegates on the committees. And, finally, the degree of need in the market may be inversely proportional to the speed with which the standard is developed. These truisms contain much of the rationale for why things appear to happen so slowly in standards.

First of all, the type of standards committee that is creating the standard greatly affects the speed of creation. A committee formed under the AO method would probably move the most quickly, since it would have the available expertise to create a standard easily. The canvass method probably would be the next most time efficient, since it presupposes consensus. Finally, an ASC would be the least time efficient, since ASCs are supposed to deal with the contentious issues.

Industry interest, reflected in the number of delegates who attend the meetings, is the next consideration. The ASC normally handles standards that attract the interest and participation of everyone in the industry. For high-interest standards that are more specific to a discipline, the AO would be better. And, finally, for a single common and understood subject, the canvass method would be best.

If the topic to be standardized is defined easily, the standardization process can be completed in a reasonable period of time. A technically bound standard dealing with a simple issue can take as little as eighteen months to complete. If the subject is complex and has multiple interpretations or large-scale economic consequences, development is likely to require substantially more time. A complete complex standard on a highly contentious issue that involves a great deal of industry participation can and should take at least five years to come into being. A standard rarely is completed in less than a year; approximately four years should be the average.

In these estimates, the term "should" is used advisedly. It carries a double meaning—first, indicating that this is the typical time, and, second, suggesting that it is desirable for a standard to take this long. The problem, of course, is the industry's ability to deal with rapid change. If standards are a change agent for the industry, in which the entire industry can compete, measured and rational change is essential. At the same time, standards are a marketing tool, which can and should be used by providers as a means to gain a market advantage. These two goals are not mutually incompatible, but they do lend an aura of tension to an already complex forum. Standards should be part of a midrange strategic plan in most corporations in the United States. As was stated in an earlier chapter, standards are not a quick fix to correct a lack of planning. The process is difficult to manage as a solution to an immediate corporate problem. It does not respond well to the frenzied cries of desperate marketing people; rather, it emphasizes and rewards careful planning and strategy.

Conclusion

The standards process is not found in many strategic plans; many businesses are unaware of the consensus standards organizations that provide standards for their industry and of the opportunities to participate in the process. As with other methods of achieving an economic advantage, the standards process requires some discipline, calculated thought, and analysis of the variables that will be encountered. Part of the analysis should include an effort to understand the process itself. This chapter covered some of the variables of the system—variables that are independent of the goodness or validity of a proposed standard. Because standards are created in the human arena, there is a large potential for random occurrences to determine the success or failure of a proposal. The process, with its multitude of implicit and explicit checks and balances, can be confusing. Ultimately, however, a proposal's success will be decided by how well it meets market requirements and needs. The process cannot ensure success for a standard, nor can it guarantee that bad standards will not exist. All the process can do—and all that it is supposed to do—is to ensure that everyone has a chance to comment upon and change a proposal to make it the best possible within the limits of the workaday world.

9 . THE FUTURE OF

CONSENSUS STANDARDS

Ah, my Belovéd, fill the Cup that clears
Today of past Regrets and future Fears.

The Rubaiyat of Omar Khayyam
Edward Fitzgerald

What constitutes success for a standards group? Too often, the functional goodness of a standards group is measured by the amount of paper it produces and its ability to create new and improved standards and to protect the hegemony of its specific discipline. Ideally, however, each standards organization should have the same goal—the continuation and growth of the industry and/or discipline that it services by ensuring that the consensus standards process is viable. Note that the goal is not the creation of standards. If a standards group never creates a single standard but provides a common forum for the industry/discipline it represents, makes available useful standards developed by other groups, and interacts freely and constructively with other organizations, then that standards group has succeeded. Success, therefore, appears to rest heavily on a group's ability to participate actively in the national and international arenas and to cooperate, when necessary, for the larger good of the discipline and/or industry.

Determining what is good for the industry—and what is meant by good—is the responsibility of each participant in the process. Market share and growth, profit, and satisfied customers, singly or in combination, are all priorities that vary from company to company, discipline to discipline, and industry to industry. Each standards group must recognize the diversity of goals and interests that confront it and learn to manage that diversity. All too often the groups are more interested in the creation of standards, which are sold to ensure the financial continuity of the group, than in the service that they render to their ultimate clients—the end users. "Good" is not necessarily more standards; probably, it is good standards that have a larger audience within the industry and help the industry as a whole.

Most of the major standards groups in the world were begun in the late 1800s or the early 1900s, although some have been created as recently as the early 1980s. Nearly all of the groups use a hierarchical structure, or slightly modified version thereof, as their basic organizational and management template. This structure has a splendid history of success in heavy industry, where there is a long tradition of slow, predictable change and the functions of each position are known and well defined. Yet both of these preconditions for success— regularity and constancy—are noticeably lacking in IT standards work. Suggestions for standards can arrive from anyone, anywhere, at any time—this is one of the major strengths of the consensus standards process. The nature of the standards business changes constantly, depending upon who is available and who has the technology. The technology changes as well, and the players, all volunteers, change rapidly, as they move from company to company, discipline to discipline, and industry to industry.

Standards organizations have responded to this change by adding layers and layers of management and coordinating committees to impose a hierarchical structure, however artificially. This has slowed the pace of change with which the standards groups have had to deal, since things (such as standards proposals) are now sitting in committee or moving slowly through several layers of management. (The principle is, if you keep extending the pipeline, nothing will ever emerge from the other end.) The price for this control, however, is very high. Standards now take an average of four years to complete; much more, if they are controversial.

The traditional providers of standards (organizations formed before

1960) now are confronting rival groups representing different points of view and ways of operating. As a result, there is a growing fracturing of the standards movement, both in Europe and the United States. The end users, the ultimate consumers of the standards, are beginning to question the usefulness of the standards that are being produced, since the fragmentation of the groups has led to multiple and redundant standards. Regulations now are beginning to lead the standards process.

In Chapter 2, regulation was described as the governmental response to civic concern, employed when the average user was incapable of effectively responding to or influencing the actions of industry. The current rash of regulatory standards (in ergonomics, software quality, and quality in general) shows that, once again, the perception has surfaced that a set of users is unable to impact the standards process in a timely manner. Whether or not the feeling is correct is immaterial: the users and, in some cases, the governments feel that the consensus standards process, which is supposed to represent all interested parties, is failing. It is this perceived lack of responsiveness, or sense of systemic failure, that is driving the activities of the new standards bodies, the governments, and the industry.

The revolt that was signaled by the Manufacturing Automation Protocol (MAP) is interesting in this context. The companies and users that formed MAP are objecting to the current practices of a standards organization; yet the form in which they have chosen to express this revolt is identical to the one to which they were objecting. In other words, MAP is a revolt not against the concept of consensus standards but against the managerial and organizational template of the standards groups that create them; its message is that the underlying principle is healthy but the application is flawed. This statement has serious implications for the future of consensus standards.

Can the consensus standards organizations regain their ability to satisfy their customers' needs and wants? I believe that it will depend on improvement in two areas: forecasting the needs—social and economic—of the users and decreasing the time from standards proposal to standards creation. Both of these are managerial problems, and both are capable of solution. Both require that the standards groups initiate a planning function, but of a nontraditional nature. The groups also must remember that they exist only to plan and make things better for the society and industry who fund them and under whose aegis they operate.

At the present time, the SDOs have broad global charters that conflict more and more as the environment changes and interdependence becomes commonplace. For these problems to be addressed, there must be decisions about which organization has hegemony, based on the status ascribed to the origins of that group, and about which nation has hegemony, since each national group represents its members and their national position as well as the industry/discipline position. For the common good, it will be necessary for each standards group to take a little less than it is claiming as its area of responsibility and sacred trust. It also will be necessary for the groups to recognize that, if each separate group claims less, the entire process will function more efficiently and increase the absolute potentiality for everyone. The question becomes, "Which group is willing to make the first sacrifice for the good of the commonweal?" Whichever group volunteers will not receive much reward for its selflessness and may even be punished for it, if the other groups take advantage of its seeming weakness instead of following its lead.

It is here that the membership of the groups themselves makes an appearance. As was noted in Chapter 6, the new standard professionals, technically competent and politically astute, are beginning to move into the standards process to represent more broadly the interests of their sponsoring organizations. These professionals will belong to more than one organization; their interests will be present in more than a single nation or region.

These interlocking interests will pose the greatest challenge to standards organizations over the next decade. They will have to dedicate time and resources to the development of a new managerial theory that takes into account the volunteer nature of the cross-organizational membership and the ability of each new professional to move and switch loyalties, acting in whatever manner seems best in the specific situation at any given moment, all while remembering that the purpose of standards is to increase commerce. It is true situational management of the most complex nature. Also of importance for the managerial study will be the impact of the various client groups on the organizations. Each SDO believes that its clients are correct in their approach to IT problem solution. As the groups become more and more interdependent, the validity of this statement is increasingly suspect, since the clients—and, more importantly, their needs—no longer seem to be absolutely clear.

It is now necessary to examine the most basic component of the standards-making organizations—the working groups, technical committees, what have you, that do the actual work of the standards world. These committees are composed of volunteers who believe enough in consensus standards to participate in the process. There is no rational explanation for why the volunteers volunteer. The work is hard and/or boring, and they must pay to do it. Macroeconomic justification, to the committee member who has just finished a seventh cup of hotel coffee during a stressful meeting, certainly has little meaning. Yet the key to the process, and to the entire standards movement, is this volunteer, who puts the standards movement at the highest risk and also offers the greatest potential for reward.

Most delegates represent personal, professional, national, disciplinary, and industry goals, all because of their personal feeling of commitment to the consensus standards process. Moreover, delegates must act in a manner that is consistent with the expectations of the committee of which they are members. If a delegate is good, he or she may influence the process positively—by participation, by reassurance, by the very act of being there. By extension, however, if the participant is not good or is not backed sufficiently by his or her sponsor, damage can occur—to the individual, to the supporting or funding organization, and to the process itself.

This is the major long-term danger to the concept of consensus standards both nationally and internationally. The best defense, obviously, is for the sponsors automatically to assign knowledgeable people to the process. The users and corporations that are the most impacted by standards must support them with competent people. A standards meeting is no longer an excuse for an entertaining trip or a place to send someone to pay back a favor or someone who can't do anything else. Nor should providers and users justify their lack of participation on the grounds that standards will get done without them somehow. (This is true, of course, but the results may come as a shock.) Standards is a discipline that has its own set of professional requirements and needs. The refusal—or inability—of corporations and user groups to understand the basic nature of standards and to use the standards groups for commerce has the potential to become a major problem over the next decade. The misuse of standards by special-interest groups and the government poses another threat to standards and the standardization process.

Implications of growth

In a market that is growing explosively and is dynamic to the point of instability, internal relationships are unclear, and there are no guarantees that tomorrow's market will be based on today's activities. In this atmosphere, planning is impossible; it is a speculator's market. No standards can be written for this type of environment: standards are postulated on a recognized growth path and a certain continuity of progress; in a high-growth, highly dynamic market, there is nothing but discontinuity. If standards, voluntary or otherwise, are introduced into this environment, they will fail, since standards act to stabilize a market.

Conversely, in a market where growth largely has ceased and where the internal dynamics are regularized, there is little opportunity for standards to make a contribution. When the industry relationships are known and the attributes of the market are clear, the market already has attained the stability that standards might have offered. In these instances, standards serve only to clarify the attributes of both the industry and market and tend to slow the market dynamics even more. It is here that "perfect" standards are written. In effect, the industry is proclaiming its fatigue by having rules substitute for originality and order substitute for growth.

In both of these markets, standards are unnecessary, because, for very different reasons, they cannot fill the function for which they are best suited. Standards need a setting in which they can provide some stability without becoming moribund. And this is tied to the growth of the standards activities in an industry itself.

The information technology industry is growing—more people than ever before are using the products of the industry, and those products are reaching more and more areas. The dynamic nature of this market makes the voluntary standards groups even more necessary. It has become too expensive to support random growth, and the growing interdependence of the various portions of the market have acted as a further inducement for standards. Standards provide a visible metric against which vendors can compare the performance of their products. Additionally, the standards provide a launch platform for future attempts to improve products or concepts. The use of standards furnishes the market with a free lengthening of the product life cycle. They provide an essential gestation period for products under development, when concepts and products can be evaluated and tested, then corrected if necessary or offered without change, depending upon the response of one's peers in the standards community.

Each standards-setting group has established an area of expertise and grown in that area. Over the years, the groups have expanded their islands of influence, until now the islands have become dangerously close and, in a few instances, actually touched. This is the predicament that we have today in standards, discussed earlier in this chapter. Yet, while this growth has caused problems, it also has added purpose and impetus to standards activities. The standards groups must respond quickly to the changing needs of the market and industry, lest they be left behind. At the same time, the demands of change require standards organizations to give up the goal of perfect standards and concentrate instead on producing working solutions to the problems confronting the industry.

The industry growth thus has proved to be a mixed blessing. It got the standards groups out from under their tamarind tree and made them necessary and vital, but it also is forcing them to confront their interdependence. This confrontation, if properly managed, will strengthen the process. If improperly managed, it will weaken the industry—at a time when significant changes are occurring nationally and internationally. I sincerely doubt that consensus standards have the power to cause fundamental changes in the way that capitalism and the governments interrelate, but I do feel that the information technology industry is a major social and cultural force within society. Because consensus standards are part of the IT industry, their failure and its concomitant impact on the IT industry probably would ripple throughout society as a whole.

A failure of the consensus standards program to achieve internal coordination of its own activities will result in its own removal; it will be replaced by a more efficient and workable method of setting industry and market standards. I have a fondness for the present method; I would prefer to see it survive. Certainly, I believe that standards and standards organizations will continue and will prosper—there will always be someone or something creating standards in the world. At the same time, there will always be someone or something that objects to current standards, standards organizations, and standards processes and will fight to change or improve them. The question is, what form will this objection take? Ultimately, it boils down to whether the change in standards, standards organizations, and their processes will be evolutionary or revolutionary.

I believe that, as time passes, the national organizations—including the professional and user groups—will become more and more focused on their role in international organizations and will attempt to increase their ability to impact—for better or for worse—international standards. There will be a gradual evolutionary movement away from the consensus system as it appears today, toward greater participation in single national forums. The speed of decision making will not increase substantially; planning and consideration of standards activities long before they are actual, however, will increase. This effort to make standards organizations more long-range focused and more planning oriented will constitute the major change in standards organizations over the next decade.

PART III. CURRENT
STANDARDS ORGANIZATIONS

1 0 . I N T E R N A T I O N A L

S T A N D A R D S   B O D I E S

> By me, the hemispheres rounded and tied
> The unknown to the known.
>
> *Prayer of Columbus*
> Walt Whitman

The three senior international standards bodies that impact the information technology field will be examined in this chapter: the International Organization for Standardization (ISO), the International Electrotechnical Commission (IEC), and the International Telecommunication Union (ITU). Each of these organizations produces standards or recommendations using a form of voluntary process and has a distinct, although sometimes overlapping, area of interest and activity. To provide the necessary context for the activities of the IT committees, the organizational structure, rules, and procedures their parent committees will be examined where appropriate.

The International Organization for Standardization (ISO)

The International Organization for Standardization (ISO), established in 1946, is a completely voluntary organization, the result of free and open agreement among nations—and the organizations that represent national standardization interests—to recognize the hegemony of a single organization and to attempt to coordinate standardization efforts to encourage lessening of national prejudices. Unlike the other organizations discussed in this chapter, ISO is not concerned with a single discipline but with "industrial standards," which cover areas ranging from mica (Technical Committee 56), to boilers and pressure vessels (Technical Committee 11), to information-processing systems (Joint Technical Committee 1). The purpose of ISO is to facilitate the international interchange of goods and services, and to encourage cooperation in economic, intellectual, technological, and scientific endeavors. It is this broad range of interests and concerns that qualifies ISO as the premier standards organization in the world.

ISO's range of interests is explained by its membership, which comprises the national organizations believed to be the most representative standards bodies of the various participating nations. (Because each organization must represent all the interests of its nation across the board in the international forum, a national group representing only one discipline quickly would put its country at a disadvantage.) However, ISO does not have standards authority in two important areas: telecommunications belong to the ITU, and electrical and electronic engineering standards are the preserve of the IEC, although, as IT becomes more and more intertwined with electronic engineering, the differences between some of the standards efforts of the IEC and ISO have become blurred over time. The ISO/IEC Joint Technical Committee 1 is a committee composed of both ISO and IEC technical committees merged into one very large standards committee, charged with standardization of information technology systems. In matters of electrical engineering, such as wiring schema, electrical safety, and electrical technical details not associated with IT equipment, the IEC remains the authority. Likewise, the ITU is the authority in telecommunications, although, again, there are increasing numbers of liaisons between it and JTC 1 committees.

Some numbers will give an indication of the enormous scope of ISO's standardization activities. There are approximately 2400 committees, subcommittees, working groups, and study groups in ISO; since 1947, ISO groups have published over 6700 international standards; 20,000 participants are involved actively in technical committee work; and, finally, on any working day of the year, there will be at least nine ISO technical meetings in progress somewhere in the world.

ISO: Membership and organization

There are two types of membership associated with ISO. The first is the "member body," which is the "organization that is most representative of standardization within its country." In this form of membership, an organization (and hence its nation) may participate with full voting rights in any ISO technical committee or subcommittee, is eligible for Council membership, and has the right to be seated in the General Assembly. Of the eighty-seven organizations participating in ISO, seventy-four are member bodies. It should be noted that over 70 percent of member bodies are governmental institutions or organizations that are incorporated under public law. In nearly every case, member bodies have close ties with organizations considered to represent national interests and usually vote, or are perceived as voting, according to the national will.

The second form of membership is the "correspondent member," usually a governmental organization of a developing country. In this case, the country has no standardization organization but sends a governmental group to keep track of the activities of ISO. Correspondent members do not take an active part in the technical groups, nor do they have the right to vote in the General Assembly, although they may attend the General Assembly as observers.

The organizational structure of ISO is shown in Figure 10-1. The General Assembly (GA), charged with making all of the policy decisions of ISO, is the highest policy body of the organization. However, because the General Assembly meets only once every three years, the strategy necessary to implement its policy decisions is managed by the Council, which is composed of the president of the General Assembly (who is the chairperson), the GA vice president, the treasurer, and eighteen other elected officers from the member bodies. This group is charged further with deciding the technical structure of

Figure 10-1. Organizational structure of ISO

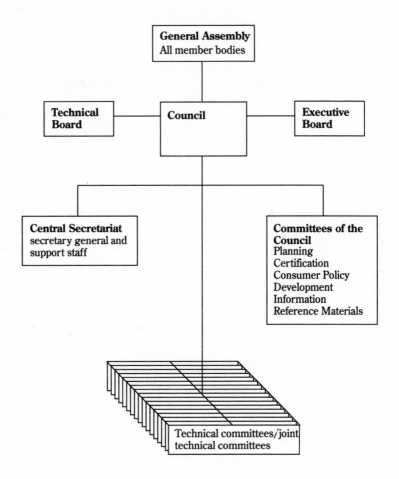

ISO, accepting approved standards for publication, and appointing the members of the Executive and Technical Boards and the chairpersons of the technical committees.

The Council meets only once a year, so the Executive Board and the Technical Board are charged with various responsibilities to ensure the smooth running of ISO. The Executive Board's mission is to assist the Council on matters of administration and organization, to oversee the budget process, and generally to see that the strategy is translated into a viable tactical action plan. The Executive Board also appoints chairpersons to the technical committees in the absence of the Council. The Technical Board is responsible to the Council for technical matters relating to ISO standards, including definition of scope and the programs that ISO will undertake, as well as establishing new committees in the absence of the Council. A number of technical advisory groups report to the Technical Board on certain areas of technology that the board feels need monitoring.

Next, six standing committees of the Council focus on the administrative and developmental aspects of standardization and standardization's impact, rather than on standards themselves. These groups are attempting to fulfill a secondary responsibility of standardization that largely has been overlooked in the past—the need to answer the question, "Now that you've got it, what are you going to do with it?"

Finally, there are the joint ISO/IEC (or IEC/ISO) groups that are studying ways to ensure that the two organizations work together peacefully and harmoniously.

The glue that holds all of this activity together is the Central Secretariat of ISO. The Central Secretariat, located in Geneva, is composed of approximately 140 people and is responsible for ensuring that the activities of ISO make sense, that the 164 technical committees do not interfere with one another, that the eighty-seven member nations are aware of what is happening, and that the mini-UN that ISO is survives and prospers. However, since the basic function of a standards organization is to cause standards to be produced, the Central Secretariat must also respond to the needs of the Secretariats of the 164 technical committees—the groups that are responsible for managing the volunteers who write the standards.

The technical committee (TC) is the key to the success of ISO. Each major topic for standardization is examined to see if it applies to a current committee. If it can be assigned, it is; if it cannot be assigned to a current committee and there is sufficient interest in the topic, a new committee will be formed. The committees are numbered in chronological order upon creation—in other words, TC 25 antedates TC 26. When a committee is disbanded or merged, its number is not reassigned. The committees, as of this writing, are numbered up to TC 191 (Humane Animal Traps), with twenty-seven TCs having been dissolved over the years. TC 1, begun in 1947, dealt with screw threads.

Each technical committee has a Secretariat assigned from one of the member bodies. (Member bodies must volunteer to sponsor Secretariats; they are somewhat expensive to maintain.) Each TC Secretariat is responsible to the Central Secretariat of ISO for ensuring that all of the necessary checks and balances of the consensus standards methodology are followed and that the activities of the TC proceed smoothly. Each TC can have subcommittees (SCs), which also must have Secretariats (again, from member bodies, that, again, carry an administrative cost) that are responsible for the subcommittees' activities. Finally, each TC and SC can have working groups (WGs). WGs do not have Secretariats, using Conveners (who must belong to a member body) instead. Each TC Secretariat is responsible for maintaining a liaison with other TCs that might be impacted by its work.

Any member body of ISO can request representation on any TC, SC, or WG. This representation can come in either of two forms— participant (P-Member) or observer (O-Member). O-Members are simply kept informed of the work of the TC, SC, or WG, whereas P-Members must take an active part in the creation of the standard by attending meetings and voting on the standard issues. Furthermore, only a P-Member may serve as the Secretariat of a TC or an SC.

ISO: Procedures

The process of creating an international standard is relatively lengthy, but it ensures that consensus is reached. However, in the case of a contentious or complex subject, especially, the leadership and the membership of the originating committee become vitally important if the proposed standard is not to die in internecine wars.

A proposal for a new work item (NWI) is drafted by a P-member, SC, or liaison organization and submitted to a TC for ballot for acceptance. If it passes this first hurdle, it is assigned to an SC for standardization activity. Usually, a WG of the SC creates a Working Draft (WD) and forwards it to the SC for vote. If the SC vote indicates that consensus has been achieved, the WD become a Draft Proposal (DP), which is then registered and circulated to the full TC. If there is consensus on the DP, it is forwarded to the Central Secretariat for registration as a Draft International Standard (DIS). The Central Secretariat verifies that the DIS meets the requirements of an ISO standard and then circulates it among ISO members for their review and approval; again, consensus is of paramount importance. After receiving the approval of a majority of TC members and 75 percent of ISO voting members, the standard is submitted to the Council for publication as an International Standard (IS).

ISO-IEC Joint Technical Committee 1 (JTC 1)

Many of ISO's technical committees are involved in some way with information technology. However, only one has the charter to deal primarily with information technology—Joint Technical Committee 1. As of 1989, JTC 1 had twenty-two P-Members and seventeen O-Members, sixteen SCs (and their Secretariats), sixty-two WGs, nine ISO TCs with which liaison was maintained, and seven IEC TCs that also required liaison. JTC 1 was formed in 1987—created from an amalgam of ISO Technical Committee 97 (formerly ISO's IT technical committee) and two IEC committees (TC 47B and TC 83), which also were concerned with IT standardization. Since most of the activity within JTC 1 is based on activity formerly in TC 97, a look at that now-defunct committee will provide a context within which to view JTC 1.

TC 97 was created in 1960, partly in response to the proposed creation of ASC X3, to standardize "computers and information processing," although its charter later was expanded to include computers, peripherals, and computer systems. Its Secretariat was offered to ANSI, which accepted with alacrity. Slightly earlier in the same year, TC 95 had been formed to deal with office machines, which were still relatively distinct from computers at the time (at least there was a perceived difference). By 1981, however, this distinction had blurred, and TC 95, which had accomplished most of what it had been chartered to do in 1961, was merged into TC 97, with 95 becoming one of the twenty-seven retired committee numbers. Further integration occurred in 1983, when two TC 97 subcommittees (SC 8, Numerical Control of Machines, and SC 9, Programming Languages for Numerical Control) were spun off to create a new ISO Technical Committee—TC 184, Industrial Automation Systems.

In 1984, TC 97 was reorganized to make it more responsive to the needs of the information technology industry. The scope of the committee was changed to "standardization, including terminology, in the field of information processing systems including, but not limited to, personal computers and office equipment." The various committees in TC 97 were modified, and an effort was made to compartmentalize (or at least group) like activities through the appointment of three vice-chairpersons, each of whom was responsible for coordinating the activities of a group of SCs with similar interests. The three groups were Application Elements (SC 1, SC 7, SC 14, and SC 22), Equipment and Media (SC 10, SC 11, SC 13, SC 15, SC 17, SC 19, and SC 23), and Systems (SC 2, SC 6, SC 18, SC 20, and SC 21). As this reorganization took place, there was an adjustment to the SCs themselves, involving the phasing out of SC 16 (Open Systems Interconnection), SC 5 (Programming Languages), and SC 12 (Instrumentation Magnetic Tape) and the creation of SC 21 (Information Retrieval,

Transfer, and Management for Open Systems Interconnection), SC 22 (Application Systems Environments and Programming Languages), and SC 23 (Optical Digital Data Disks).

In 1987, after several years of discussions, meetings, and conferences, ISO and the IEC agreed to create a joint technical committee that would be responsible for IT standards. The increasing overlap of the two groups' standardization activities in this area had the potential for producing incompatible standards for the same device or product, and the volunteers who served on the committees creating the standards were pressing both organizations to come to a compromise for the good of the industry. This led to the establishment of the Joint Technical Committee 1 of ISO/IEC, with the scope of "standardization in the field of information technology."

The Secretariat of the committee was offered to the United States (ANSI). After some discussion within ANSI on the benefits that this valuable, if expensive, Secretariat conferred upon the United States, a majority of ANSI's membership came to realize that having the Secretariat in the United States would be of major importance to the national standards effort and well worth the cost to the U.S. national standards associations and members.

To mitigate the impact of the change, much of what had been TC 97 was retained, although the three-part structure of TC 97 was recast in four parts to facilitate the integration of the IEC and ISO groups. The four new groups were Application Elements, Equipment and Media, Systems Support, and Systems.

The organization of JTC 1 and its subcommittees is shown in Figure 10-2. Note that the committees do not report to their vice-chairs; the vice-chair is an administrative function imposed upon the organization so that the chair is not overwhelmed by the job of managing the interrelations of seventeen committees. To ensure that the "six interacting entities" concept of the "span of control" is observed, the vice-chairs coordinate the activities of their subgroups; the chair then has only to coordinate the activities of the vice-chairs.

The Advisory Group to JTC 1 acts as a steering committee when

Figure 10-2. Organizational structure of JTC 1

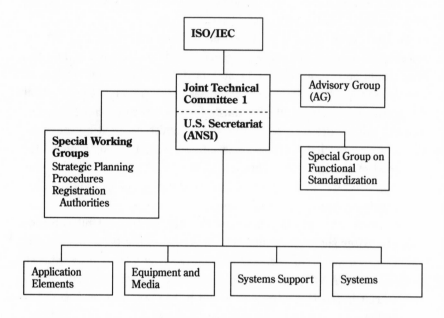

decisions or guidance is needed. It assists the chair and Secretariat in their duties and aids in the resolution of intercommittee discussions. It helps to assign responsibilities to the SCs, coordinates meetings, interfaces where necessary with standards groups external to JTC 1, and makes recommendations for new work areas. In effect, the AG performs the JTC 1 staff functions.

Four Special Working Groups (SWG) report to JTC 1. Strategic Planning operates under the auspices of the Advisory Group and is charged with assuring that the various SCs' planning is coordinated to some extent—or at least does not disagree too violently. Procedures is charged with dealing with ISO and the IEC and attempting to develop harmonized procedures, as well as reviewing and monitoring the procedural documents of JTC 1. Registration Authorities operates under the auspices of the AG and focuses on the requirement for registration that may be contained in technical standards. In effect, this group makes sure that a standard that mentions a registration authority does so correctly, in accordance with the rules covering registration. Finally, Application Portability is charged with investigating the SSI problem and reporting their findings and recommendations to the Advisory Group.

Another separate body, the Special Group on Functional Standards, was created to deal with Functional Standards and to advise JTC 1 on the issues of International Standardized Profiles.

The area of responsibility, title, and nation holding the Secretariat of each SC are shown in Figure 10-3.

The purpose of JTC 1 is to see that an international vehicle is available to aid in the standardization of "information processing systems." Its existence is predicated on understanding what a standard is expected to provide and whom it will benefit. It all turns on the thesis that a standard is a workable piece of technology—a solution that may not be technically superior but is an acceptable response to the technical and business problems that caused its creation.

While JTC 1 has a mandated international focus, each delegate has a national focus, representing her or his country in the international

135

Figure 10-3. Committee of JTC 1

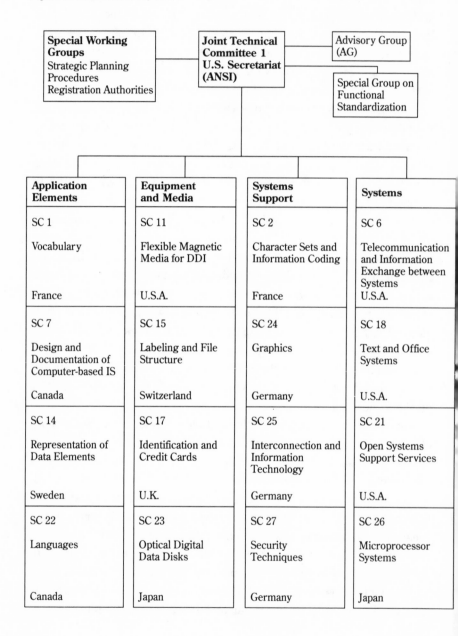

Special Working Groups Strategic Planning Procedures Registration Authorities	Joint Technical Committee 1 U.S. Secretariat (ANSI)	Advisory Group (AG) Special Group on Functional Standardization

Application Elements	Equipment and Media	Systems Support	Systems
SC 1 Vocabulary France	SC 11 Flexible Magnetic Media for DDI U.S.A.	SC 2 Character Sets and Information Coding France	SC 6 Telecommunication and Information Exchange between Systems U.S.A.
SC 7 Design and Documentation of Computer-based IS Canada	SC 15 Labeling and File Structure Switzerland	SC 24 Graphics Germany	SC 18 Text and Office Systems U.S.A.
SC 14 Representation of Data Elements Sweden	SC 17 Identification and Credit Cards U.K.	SC 25 Interconnection and Information Technology Germany	SC 21 Open Systems Support Services U.S.A.
SC 22 Languages Canada	SC 23 Optical Digital Data Disks Japan	SC 27 Security Techniques Germany	SC 26 Microprocessor Systems Japan

forum. Although the bylaws of JTC 1 do not require every participant to attend all meetings, it is necessary if one is a P-member of the committee and is recommended if a delegate is to represent effectively the national interests that he or she is charged to uphold. The dynamics of a given meeting are vital to understanding the activities and positions that are taken by the various delegates. This representation is expensive, however—all delegates pay all of their expenses. Meetings are held from Tokyo to Brighton to New York, and a delegate must either be personally wealthy or have a sponsor with deep pockets. Because attendance is as costly as it is worthwhile, it is usually logical to send the best delegate (technically, politically, organizationally) that one has available to guarantee a return on expenses. Most delegates to JTC 1, in fact, are standards professionals who understand the intricacies and complexities of standards development.

Based on this, it is reasonable to assume that JTC 1 representatives work from three fundamental perspectives. First, they tend to be biased in favor of the national governments that they represent. While the delegates are all skilled professionals who share the same vocabulary of the IT industry and standards, they all represent their nations—and are seated with national delegations—at JTC 1 meetings. Second, all representatives incline toward the point of view of the IT industry—that is, one of their most fundamental concerns is the information technology industry and its growth. Finally, a majority of the members represent sponsors and so look at their activity in standards in very pragmatic terms, since they are charged by their sponsors to provide a return on the investment represented by their participation in the standards process. (It should be noted that the nature of the sponsorship itself can impact this bias. Although a preponderance of members come from companies within the industry, a standards professional can be sponsored by an organization other than a corporation, such as a school or a government, with an interest in seeing something done in a particular way. In these cases, the bias involves advocacy of a national interest or a technical methodology peculiar to a school.) Still, the scope of ISO and JTC 1 is so broad, a global view of the standardization process has tended to make the members more tolerant of the systems complexities of information technology and more aware of the end user of the standards. The members of JTC 1 can be said to look at standards first from a national viewpoint, then from the viewpoint of the standards profession (and all that this implies), and then to proceed through the interests of the sponsors and the industry to arrive finally at an international perspective.

Because of the individual variability of these underlying motivations, the committees of JTC 1 reflect the increasing importance of "common systemness" in standards. This need for systemness—or interoperability—is especially visible in the Systems Group of JTC 1, which is responsible for developing the Open Systems Interconnect (OSI) model for JTC 1. The pursuit of systemness is driven by the industry: by users, who want a degree of vendor independence; by governments, who support national processes, needs, and manufacturers; and, most urgently, by manufacturers, who want to be able to compete in a larger market. ("Manufacturers" here refers not only to hardware equipment manufacturers but also to systems integrators, software suppliers, and peripherals manufacturers—the entire gamut of producers necessary to conceptualize, design, produce, test, consult, and run an information technology processing system.) This breadth and depth of interest in the systemness of the OSI model is one of the most important aspects of JTC 1 and gives it its value, prestige, and power.

The International Electrotechnical Commission (IEC)

As noted in the previous section, the International Electrotechnical Commission (IEC), stands on equal footing with ISO. But, whereas ISO represents all industries, the IEC is limited by its charter to a singular discipline—that relating to electrical and electrotechnical matters. Formed in 1906, the IEC was a response to a real and perceived need to standardize in the electric and electronic fields, specifically, to control the increasing divergence of the European and North American electric power requirements—220 and 115 volts. Although the IEC was created too late to prevent this rift, it has become a force in forestalling similar situations and in minimizing their economic impact if they do occur.

The IEC focuses on the technical aspects of electricity—measurement, testing, utilization, and safety. It is concerned with producing "specification standards," which detail the minimum set of acceptable features that each product must conform to or be tested against. (A product may exceed the minimum standards and remain acceptable.) These standards provide a criterion for evaluation—if a product conforms to a standard, it is recognized as having a distinct set of features that quantify its value. This quantification allows users and manufacturers to understand what they have, to know that the designs and safety features have been proven (or at least tested) and that a common methodology may be used to accomplish a technical electrical task.

IEC: Membership and organization

The IEC, like ISO, is a voluntary organization, composed of national members who represent the interests of their countries but who also represent the users, manufacturers, trade associations, government, and academic associations within that country. The commission has forty-two national committees, and a Registered Subscriber Service allows national entities with no national committee to remain informed of what the IEC is doing.

The organization of the IEC is shown in Figure 10-4. The structure is similar to that of ISO, with a General Assembly, Council, Committee for Action, technical committees, and subcommittees, although an important difference is that the Committee for Action is the focus of communication, rather than the Council, which acts as the IEC's governing board. This provides for more centralized communication, since the Committee for Action is also responsible for acting on technical requests for standards and allocating them to TCs or SCs for

Figure 10-4. Organizational structure of the IEC

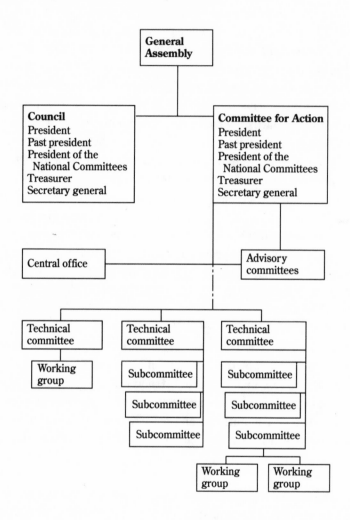

action. The members of the Committee for Action are elected by the Council, which usually meets in conjunction with the IEC's plenary session. (The plenary occurs yearly, attended by the heads of each national delegation accompanied by a small entourage.) Three advisory committees advise the Committee for Action when a technical topic is not covered by an existing TC or when several TCs are impacted by the topic.

The IEC uses technical committees to create its standards. Currently, there are eighty-two TCs (two are shared with ISO in JTC 1), each of which can have subcommittees. The subcommittees can have working groups if they need them. Each technical committee has a Secretariat, as does each subcommittee. In 1988, there were over 200 TCs and SCs in IEC.

A major difference between ISO and the IEC is the nature of the representation on the TCs. In the IEC, each member nation belongs to every TC, whether or not it has any interest or concern. As a result, each member nation has a stake in every emerging standard.

IEC: Procedures

The IEC standards-creation process is similar to the ISO model. A draft standard coming out of a TC is circulated to all members, who then vote on acceptance, rejection, or change. Unreturned and "No response" ballots are taken to indicate positive responses, since IEC operates under the assumption that if something bothers someone, he or she will respond. If 20 percent of the votes are found to be negative upon completion of the balloting, the proposed standard can be modified to incorporate changes and the draft recirculated, or the entire effort can begin again. The complete process for an IEC standard takes an average of eight years at this time, although improvements are expected.

The members of the IEC have a perspective similar to that of JTC 1's members, in that manufacturers are represented heavily. Yet, where JTC 1 tends to consider problems that the ultimate users will and may experience as it moves toward a systems perspective in standards, the IEC has a bias toward the product concept, and its concerns revolve specifically around electricity and its application and use as an entity. IEC standards focus on the manufacturer of the product and are intended to ensure interoperability by providing a comparison metric, rather than a metric for interconnection performance. This emphasis has validity: there is a need for everyone in the industry to attach similar meanings to terms such as "ohm," "amp," and "volt"; without IEC standards, the common vocabulary, upon which systems understanding is built, would not exist. The IEC bias, then, is nearly the same as that of JTC 1, except that its second most important perspective is that of industry and company, followed by standards and international interests.

The International Telecommunication Union (ITU)

The International Telecommunication Union (ITU), one of the few organizations covered in this book that is not a voluntary standards group, is a formal treaty organization, organized and run under the auspices of the United Nations. As a treaty organization, the ITU has the right and duty to set international regulatory standards, which are administered by governments rather than industries. If a government, as a national entity, accepts the positions of the ITU, it proposes regulations, backed by both positive and negative sanctions, to impose the standards within its jurisdiction. The seriousness with which the regulations are regarded can be judged by the mechanisms employed by the national government to enforce them. The area of jurisdiction of the ITU, simply stated, is all telecommunications usage—planning, regulating, coordinating, and standardizing.

The ITU Convention recognizes three purposes for the organization: to maintain and extend cooperation in the *development and use of telecommunications* (italics added) between present members (and to help developing nations); to promote the development of technical facilities to improve the *efficiency of telecommunications* (italics added); and to harmonize the actions of nations to attain these two goals. To meet these aims, the ITU allocates radio frequencies, coordinates efforts to eliminate radio interference between nations, helps developing nations use telecommunications technology, advises members on rate setting so that they remain fiscally viable while serving their communities, looks at safety-of-life issues as they relate to telecommunications, and undertakes studies, makes regulations, adopts resolutions, and collects and publishes information on telecommunications matters.

ITU: Membership and organization

The ITU consists of 160 member nations, each of which signs the ITU Convention at the Plenipotentiary Conference, held on an irregular basis every five to nine years. The Plenipotentiary Conference, like the ISO General Assembly, sets broad policy and objectives, called the Articles of Convention. It also oversees the election of the Administrative Council, which meets annually to deal with administrative matters for the conference. Because the ITU is a treaty organization, member nations usually are represented by an agency of the government. In the United States, that agency is the State Department. In most other countries, it is the national PTT, the organization in charge of postal, telegraph, and telephone services.

Figure 10-5 shows an ITU organizational schematic. Administrative Councils, which meet either regionally or internationally at the request of member nations, have a shorter time focus and are used by the ITU to deal with the more specific issues at hand. They function in a fashion similar to ISO's Executive Board or the IEC's Committee for Action. There are also four permanent committees assigned to the ITU: the General Secretariat, providing administrative support and technical help to developing nations, the International Frequency Registration Board (IFRB), the International Radio Consultative Committee (CCIR), and the International Telegraph and Telephone Consultative Committee (CCITT), the ITU organization of importance to information technology.

Figure 10-5. Organizational structure of the ITU

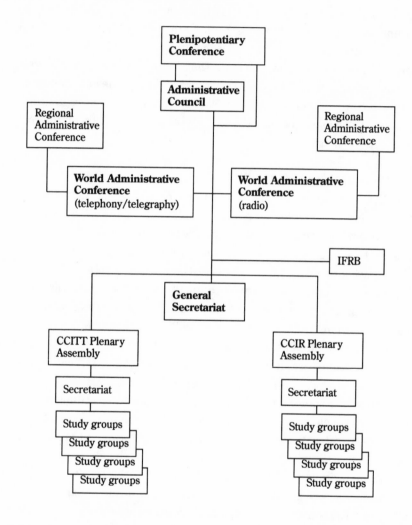

ITU: Procedures

In the time between its Plenipotentiary Conferences, the ITU develops and creates radio, telegraph, and telephone regulations, which are binding upon the nations that accept them, since the ITU has international treaty status. However, these regulations are used only for vital issues; more numerous are the CCITT Recommendations offering technical and operational standards, tariffs, administrative directives, and terminology statements. These Recommendations are exactly that—recommendations—and are not binding but usually are used as the basis for any negotiations and agreements. In addition, technical Recommendations have a way of becoming *de facto* international standards, since they provide technical insight on how to connect to the international telecommunications system.

International Telegraph and Telephone Consultative Committee (CCITT)

Founded in 1956 and headquartered in Geneva, the CCITT is to the ITU what JTC 1 is to ISO, although I am not sure that members of either organization would welcome the comparison. While there are outstanding differences between the two groups (voluntary versus treaty, voluntary standards versus Recommendations), each serves the same function for its parent organization—to help standardize the information technology area, a difficult and time-consuming chore that is nonetheless growing very rapidly and is perilous to ignore.

There are four classes of membership in the CCITT. Administration membership, open to any of the ITU's 160 members, confers one vote to each member on the unusual occasions when a vote is required. The next form of membership is that of the Recognized Private Operating Agencies (RPOAs), which have full membership as the basic telecommunication service providers for the world; there are fifty-eight such organizations in CCITT. The next category of membership includes the Scientific or Industrial Organizations (SIOs), which provide a base of technical expertise to the organization. The SIOs are not invited to Plenary sessions but often heavily influence the CCITT

Recommendations. SIOs, of which there are presently 146, must have the approval of their governments in order to participate. Finally, the major international organizations, such as the IEC and ISO, are invited to attend meetings to ensure that they are aware of what the CCITT is doing. There are thirty-six members of this type in 1988.

The CCITT does the bulk of its work in study groups (SG), which are further subdivided into working parties (WP). Questions are formulated during the Plenary Assembly and then given to the appropriate SGs for study. As an SG pursues its work, members are encouraged to make contributions, which form the basis of Recommendations. These Recommendations, the result of consensus among the members of the affected SGs and WPs, are then sent to the Plenary Assembly, which alone has the power to accept or reject them. Since Plenary Assemblies are held only every four years, an SG may request that the CCITT ballot members to allow a provisional Recommendation to be established. Provisional Recommendations are, of course, subject to approval at the next Plenary.

Most relevant to the information technology industry is CCITT Study Group VII (Data Communications Networks), with lesser input coming from SGs VIII (Terminal Equipment for Telematic Services) and XVIII (Digital Networks, including ISDN). SG VII's influence stems from its work on Open Systems Interconnect, which is a major effort in ISO/IEC JTC 1, especially in SC 21. Furthermore, there is an increasing intersection between the information-processing functions of JTC 1 and the telecommunication function of the CCITT.

The primary responsibility of the CCITT, however, continues to be telecommunications. This focus on a singular discipline, coupled with the nature of the full members (governmental administrations and service providers, which, in many countries, are one and the same), gives the CCITT its perspective. Simply put, the CCITT perceives telecommunications as an entity in and of itself, rather than as a subsystem component of information technology. This perspective is international, representing a consensus of all national entities and national telecommunications providers. Finally, as part of an organization that has official treaty status, the CCITT can produce regulations that a national governmental power can and will impose and enforce through sanctions.

Summary and conclusion

The groups described in this chapter all use essentially similar methods and structures to create standards or recommendations. All three organizations go to great pains to avoid making unilateral decisions, which, after all, could cause a loss of membership and the creation of alternate standards bodies. The use of the concept of consensus probably is most highly developed in the ITU, which deals with sovereign national governments. Next in line is ISO with its consensus-driven standards, followed by the IEC with its high majority standards. However, all three focus on the nation-state as a primary unit of judgment, and, while this is valid for a large homogeneous nation, it can be disastrous for small heterogeneous nations on large continents. Furthermore, the presumption that a national government speaks for all national interests may not be valid in some instances.

Of the five functions of management described in Chapter 7, these three international organizations seem to possess equal competence in organizing, controlling, and internal controlling (coordinating). (I omit command since it is measurable only in retrospect and is therefore a judgment call at this time.) Only planning, possibly the most critical function of all, remains an unknown. And it is here that each organization, with its unique perspectives, has the longest way to go. Each group carries the prejudices and expectations of its volunteer members. And, in turn, all of the volunteer members bring to the organization the prejudices and expectations of their sponsoring company or group, their discipline or specialty, and their national aspirations. To complicate matters further, the groups meet as semiadversaries when there are genuine disputes in interpretation and usage expectation.

While ISO can choose its members from the broadest base, it tends to think in terms of industrial standards, emphasizing the use of standards as a method of international interchange of goods and services, and to encourage cooperation in economic, intellectual, technological, and scientific endeavors. It looks at standards from the position of the major *systems* manufacturers that can influence the range of decisions that the national committees of ISO must make. The IEC does not have ISO's broad base of interests but looks more deeply at standards from a discrete electrotechnical *manufacturing* viewpoint. And, finally, the ITU looks at its activities from a telecommunications—and monopoly tariff—point of view.

The three viewpoints, while not totally exclusive, are hard to reconcile. Consensus is difficult enough to achieve within a single organization of individuals with a similar background. However—and this is the key to the entire standards process—when the three groups achieve consensus, it is likely to be synergistic, in that the resulting solution is safer, better, and more efficient than any single organization could have achieved. The price for the solution, however, is hard work and time.

11. REGIONAL

STANDARDS BODIES

> What dull men are those who tarry at home,
> When abroad they might wantonly roam,
> And gain such experience, and spy too,
> Such countries and wonders, as I do!
>
> *Cheer Up, My Mates*
> Abraham Cowley

The regional group acts as an intermediary between the international organization with its global focus and the national organization with its more intense, but narrower, concerns. A regional organization provides a national group an area in which to make proposals to potentially like-minded national organizations before taking these proposals to an international forum. Similarly, regional organizations provide the international organization the chance to sample the opinion of a group of nations without actually involving national pride and causing chauvinism to rear its head. Finally, a regional group can gain significant influence at the international level as a concentrated lobbying force.

The European Computer Manufacturers Association (ECMA)

The European Computer Manufacturers Association (ECMA) is, as its name suggests, an organization with a European regional focus whose primary clients are the computer manufacturers of Europe. It is an association that believes that the creation of regional voluntary standards for the European information technology community can bring about a larger influence for the European information technology *manufacturers*. Its purpose, then, is to increase the use of information technology products, especially those of European manufacture, to standardize these products (in cooperation with the appropriate national and international agencies), and to promulgate these standards. The organization, which is nonprofit, is prohibited by its bylaws from engaging in commercial activity, although the definition of "commercial activity" is somewhat idiosyncratic, since ECMA's activities definitely are not altruistic. Even so, ECMA has prompted European manufacturers to work together and to produce a standards product that probably is superior to any that they would have produced for a national market only.

ECMA was initiated formally in 1960, when several major computer vendors invited all known computer manufacturers in the European area to participate in a meeting to be held in April of that year. This meeting, which took place in Brussels, concluded with the recommendation that an association known as the European Computer Manufacturers Association be created and the formation of a committee to draw up the necessary bylaws for the creation of the organization.

The dynamics of ECMA's formation are interesting from a historical perspective. The three major information-processing standards groups—ISO's TC 97, ANSI's X3, and ECMA—were formed at about the same time (1960/1961), and, within this same time frame, those in data processing (later known as information technology) first began to understand some of its capabilities—and some of its problems. The capabilities were variously perceived, but it was becoming rapidly apparent that data processing was extending beyond the accounting department and moving into prominence in both corporate and academic environments. Additionally, governments were growing interested in the capabilities of data processing, from both a technical and legislative point of view. The realization of data processing's potential—coupled with the realization that this potential would diminish if some form of standardization were not put in place—led to the creation of these committees

The ostensible rationale for standardization was to help users save resources (money and people) by providing a limited degree of interoperability for systems interfaces such as input/output codes and programming languages. Further, standardization would allow users to become more familiar with the capabilities of computers, thereby making computers less frightening. However, since standards grow from some larger economic rationale, ECMA clearly was responding to the needs of the manufacturers that composed its user (or client) base. ECMA's goals were to ensure the survival of the European point of view in data processing, including the specialized needs of the various manufacturers, to see that the market expanded at a rate that would guarantee financial success for the efficient members, and to defend against any structuring of the market that would preclude substantial participation by European manufacturers. Assuring a consensus among European manufacturers through the production of standards that reflected the community of interests made it more certain that the European perspective would be heard.

In addition, ECMA was founded to act as a group that would speak for all of the European manufacturers to the European nations. National governments had begun to evolve separate standards that they believed would serve their separate national interests and effectively could function as nontariff trade barriers. The establishment of such national standards would have fragmented the European market, destroying any possibility of market potential for non-national manufacturers and severely limiting the potential gain for national manufacturers. To prevent this, manufacturers needed to create a supranational body that retained a distinctly European cast.

Standards did not have to be similar—merely compatible. It is possible to write a standard with multiple subsets to satisfy different national requirements. Such standards sometimes can be expensive to implement completely but far less so than implementing a different product for each country. Regional standards would allow a company to pick its markets by careful implementation of a standard, or parts of a standard. The company would not necessarily have to fear being closed out of a market because it forgot something.

ECMA was fairly well defined by December of 1960. Because it was believed that the organization could complement the activities of ISO and the IEC, the new organization was located in Geneva, Switzerland. ECMA formally came into being—and began to carry out its tasks—in May of 1961. Even prior to official registration, however, it already had achieved an impressive victory when it was asked by ISO and the IEC to join a roundtable conference to discuss standardization in the computer industry. The ultimate outcome of this discussion was the creation of the TC 97 (now JTC 1) and the request that ECMA act as a liaison member to that committee.

ECMA: Membership and organization

The membership of ECMA is open to any *company* in Europe that develops, manufactures, and markets data-processing machines or machines used to process digital information. The requirements are written is such a way that any major manufacturer of information-processing equipment in Europe is eligible for membership. This was especially important to the nascent ECMA organization, since many of the major manufacturers counted upon to make ECMA a success were multinational companies based in the United States, and this phrasing would not exclude these companies from membership. It was believed that the inclusion of these companies would strengthen the role of the organization and have it truly speak for European manufacturers. To avoid potential conflict, however, it was necessary to limit each company to a single vote; otherwise, a company with multiple European subsidiaries could have overwhelmed the organization. As a result, a statement in the bylaws effectively prevents multiple subsidiaries from becoming members.

At present there are two types of membership—ordinary and associate. Ordinary members are full members, with voting rights and the right to attend meetings of any and all technical working committees (TCs), the groups that actually compose standards. Associate members, on the other hand, join to provide expertise to a technical working committee or committees; they may take part in the discussions of the General Assembly but have no voting rights. There are currently twenty-nine ordinary members and fifteen associate members. New members are accorded their appropriate membership status upon acceptance by two-thirds of the ordinary members.

The General Assembly is the highest authority of ECMA. It meets a minimum of two times a year and votes upon the standards that have been developed in the TCs. Because the General Assembly is a large group, legal and operational responsibilities are delegated to three officers who are elected from the ordinary members—a president and vice president (elected yearly and permitted to serve any number of terms, as long as no more than two are consecutive) and a treasurer who can serve indefinitely. These officers are responsible for the management of ECMA; they can commit the organization to contracts and have the right to bind ECMA to a course of action.

The Coordinating Committee is composed of six ordinary members who are elected by the General Assembly for one-year terms to advise it on technical working committees. The Coordinating Committee is charged by the General Assembly with determining when a new TC is needed and what the scope of its work should be, with nominating a provisional chairperson for the TC upon its formation, and with reviewing the progress of the TCs every six months.

And, as with all standards organizations, there is the Secretariat. The ECMA Secretariat, appointed by the General Assembly, is responsible for managing the ECMA budget, which derives from the membership fees paid by the ordinary and associate members, and for ensuring that the TCs function correctly. Upon the recommendation of the Coordinating Committee, the General Assembly can vote (by simple majority) to establish a new TC, and the Secretary General of the Secretariat will call the first meeting of the TC. The Secretariat acts as the secretary for all TC meetings, helps to create the TC's agenda, publishes minutes of the meetings, and aids in preparing the activity reports that the TC chairperson provides to the Secretary General and the Coordinating Committee every six months.

TCs are the foundation of ECMA. Membership is voluntary, open to both associate and ordinary members, who, if present, may vote on technical issues regardless of their membership status. The provisional officers appointed by the Coordinating Committee are responsible for getting the TC going and can be replaced after six months and the first three meetings. Once the TC has established itself and the requisite number of meetings have been held, the TC votes in its own leadership (chair and vice-chair), which can be elected for up to three consecutive terms. The chair is responsible for maintaining the TC focus and calendar target and prepares semiannual reports to the Secretary General and the General Assembly. In 1988, there were fourteen active technical working committees and eighteen other committees that were in the "work completed" stage. Retired committee numbers are not reassigned.

A TC has the ability to create technical groups (TGs) that are responsible to it for accomplishing part of its work. TGs are composed of a minimum of two TC members and report on their activities at each meeting of the TC. They operate along the lines of a TC.

ECMA: Procedures

TCs operate under rules of modified consensus—that is, they have the option of voting on a topic, but it is strongly recommended that they resolve problems without recourse to a vote whenever possible, so that items can be forwarded with unanimity. If voting is used to resolve an issue, a simple majority decides the outcome. Any ordinary member has the right to take an exception position to a TC's proposal and to have a minority opinion recorded.

When a TC has completed its development work on a standard, the draft standard is presented to the General Assembly. The draft standard must be circulated for at least four months before the meeting of the General Assembly at which it is to be considered for adoption. This four-month period allows members time to study the draft, to understand its implications, and to develop a corporate position on the standard. Finally, the standard is voted upon in the General

Assembly. If a two-thirds majority favors it, it becomes an ECMA standard and is made available to any interested party for use.

ECMA: Conclusion

ECMA serves as a bridge between the national interests of the European manufacturers and the international standards bodies—primarily, ISO and the IEC. It can be seen in several lights. The first, and most obvious, is that it adds a layer of confusion to the standards process: it represents a very select clientele of European manufacturers, absorbs the scarce time and resources of these manufacturers, and has a set of procedures that excludes the interests of the national and international users in general. The second, and possibly more valid, interpretation is that ECMA has unified the European manufacturers into a coherent whole, allowing them to consolidate a concept of computing that permits them to share in both economies of scale and a somewhat unified market. ECMA is not motivated by altruism and can be shortsighted at times, but it has permitted the development of a European position that is ignored at peril by all—not merely European—manufacturers.

CEN and CENELEC

These two more truly European regional committees tend to deal in areas of non-IT standardization but are active in the telecommunications arena, where they represent the PTTs and other governmental organizations. For this reason, and because they are regional standards coordinating bodies, they are of interest and influence in the IT community. Additionally, their role in the standardization activities in Europe will increase over the next decade, given the 1992 deadline for the establishment of the European Community.

Comité Européen de Normalisation (CEN)

The Comité Européen de Normalisation (CEN) is the European regional equivalent of ISO. Although the present organization dates from 1971, the idea of CEN originated in 1957. Its role in the area of IT standards is increasing as the merger of IT and telecommunications grows and as the PTTs, through their national governments, attempt to expand their influence in IT. At this time, however, CEN's presence is less evident in IT than in other disciplines.

Sixteen national standards organizations of Europe make up CEN's membership. These organizations created CEN to encourage the free trade of goods and services in Europe through the use of standards. In effect, CEN is attempting to lower nontariff trade barriers erected by the European nations with their national standards organizations. To this end, CEN does cause European standards to be published but attempts primarily to harmonize the existing standards of the member nations.

CEN is governed by a General Assembly composed of all its members. This group meets annually to set policy and direction; the actual running of the organization is left to the Secretary General, aided by a technical coordinating committee and a management committee. An unusual feature of CEN not found in the ISO organization is a subordinate body, known as CENCER, that deals with certificates of conformance to CEN standards. For standards development, CEN operates in a manner similar to that of ISO, with technical committees being created as needed to do this work.

Since it deals with the national standards bodies of the European nations, CEN has quasi-legal status; member states agree to use its published standards in preference to national standards wherever possible. Furthermore, with the European directives for conjoining EC economies by 1992, CEN has moved to a more central position. Following these directives, CEN has become increasingly involved in certification and certification test houses. This development may have relatively large implications for the IT industry. If CEN succeeds in its effort to compile a regionally accepted list of test houses, it will become a major adjudicator in the IT industry in Europe, as well as the rest of the world. It remains to be seen, however, whether certification will be based on international marketing standards or on regulatory standards.

Comité Européen de Normalisation
Electrotechnique (CENELEC)

The Comité Européen de Normalisation Electrotechnique (CENE-LEC) was formed in 1973 from the merger of two existing organizations. It is the European regional equivalent of the IEC, in that it concerns itself only with electrotechnical matters. Like CEN, it was established to help the European community lower trade barriers to facilitate trade among European nations.

Again like CEN, CENELEC is composed of sixteen national European standards groups. It is governed by its General Assembly, although day-to-day affairs are run by the Secretariat and the Secretary General. Reporting to the General Assembly are the Technical Board, which controls technical activities, and the Liaison Committee, which coordinates the aims and activities of both CENELEC and its members with those of other European regional groups. In addition, a Components Committee focuses on the harmonization of electrical components standards within the European region.

CENELEC publishes European Standards and Harmonization Documents, which its members are expected to publish as national standards or to endorse for national use. Nonharmonious national standards are expected to be withdrawn from circulation or changed to harmonize with CENELEC standards.

CEN and CENELEC: Conclusion

Although CEN and CENELEC have the same address and cooperate closely, the two organizations differ in role, expectations, and scope of activity. While the member nations of CEN and CENELEC are nearly the same, it is usual for two different national bodies to represent their nation at meetings of the two committees. The exception to this is the British Standards Institute (BSI), which acts as the U.K. representative to both organizations.

CEN and CENELEC will gain power as the popularity of standards grows and the European nations coalesce to ensure that their economies are joined as required for the 1992 appearance of the Europe Community. As conformance to quality standards grows—and as the quality mark and software ergonomics increase in importance—I believe that these two organization will become significant participants in the IT standards programs in Europe and ISO.

12 . NATIONAL

STANDARDS BODIES

> Happy the man, whose wish and care
> A few paternal acres bound,
> Content to breathe his native air
> In his own ground.
>
> *Solitude*
> Alexander Pope

This chapter looks first at the umbrella organization that manages the entire national standards effort and then examines the national organizations concerned with the creation and implementation of information technology standards. Emphasis is placed on the client base of each standards organization and the underlying philosophy that impels the SDO's activities.

The American National Standards Institute (ANSI)

The American National Standards Institute (ANSI) coordinates the myriad standards activities in the United States in areas ranging from film sizes to screw threads, from automobiles to computers. It was organized in 1918 in response to a perceived crisis: the industrialization of the United States was based on the commonality of interchangeable parts over distance, and the use of "non-standard" standards was becoming a major problem. Standards were proliferating, but none was adopted by more than a handful of manufacturers. To counter this development, five leading United States engineering societies joined forces to create the American Engineering Standards Committee. The purpose of the new group was to make sure that enough commonality existed in the standards of the various disciplines to retain (or create) a set of understood and shared terms among engineers. Codifying this body of knowledge and procedures had a major impact on the rapidly increasing industrialization of the United States.

This activity by no means was limited to the United States; industrialized nations throughout the world were pursuing similar standardization activities. The U.S. organization was unique, however, in disdaining official governmental approval, preferring to have the government as a client rather than as a sponsor. Organizational and name changes occurred in the 1920s, the 1960s, and in the 1980s, but ANSI's mission has not changed substantially since its inception.

ANSI is the primary interface with the U.S. government on matters relating to standards, providing a mechanism by which the organization and company members can make their needs and desires known to the legislative and regulatory agencies. One of its main objectives over the past years has been to encourage government procurement use of ANSI approved standards, instead of internally developed standards that are unique to the office or organization doing the procurement.

ANSI is also the recognized representative to ISO and the IEC, the two major international nontreaty standards organizations. It funds the Secretariat and several subcommittees of JTC 1, the ISO committee for information technology. ANSI's position as the United States' sole representative to these organizations derives, in large part, from the international view that ANSI is the most representative standards organization in the United States.

The mission of ANSI is *not* to develop standards but to manage and coordinate private-sector standards activities to ensure that the United States has a strong standards effort that serves the national interest. A nonprofit organization, ANSI serves all industries and users in the United States; indeed, its ultimate client is the nation. ANSI supervises the voluntary efforts of nongovernmental bodies to create standards to meet the requirements of the sponsoring industries and user organizations. The groups that sponsor and develop these standards range from professional societies to technical groups, trade associations, and various other interested groups. Where it can, ANSI also manages the standards-creation process, encouraging organizations to develop standards when a gap in the current offerings is recognized. ANSI encourages these groups to submit their proposed standards for approval as American National Standards, an endorsement that only ANSI can give. If a group chooses not to submit a standard, ANSI has no recourse—except that a standard that is not so endorsed usually receives little market acceptance in the long run.

One of ANSI's most important attributes is this ability to designate standards as national consensus standards. Approval by the institute indicates that a standards-writing group used a process that provided everyone who was directly and materially affected by a standard with an opportunity to participate in its development. The right to withhold or bestow this approval, and the economic power that it confers, allows ANSI to exercise a control over the standards process that would not exist in a free-market setting. However, the perception that ANSI can impose standards is not an accurate reflection of the ephemeral power that ANSI actually possesses. It is the consensus review by all impacted parties, from providers, through users, to the government, that is the key feature of the ANSI standards process. Under consensus, acceptance of a standard occurs when there is no compelling reason not to allow it (to phrase it another way, adoption is only possible when all parties agree that no interests are compromised by the standard). The system is highly dependent upon shared understandings and expectations, both within the community of ANSI and the society as a whole.

As a voluntary consensus standards organization, ANSI realizes that it will fail if it does not achieve consensus in its standards activities. Thus, one of its primary concerns is ensuring that a viable consensus process is followed. As a basic rule, it will not list as a national standard any standard that has not been through its established mechanism for obtaining consensus. This includes using the concept of due process, which allows any interested or impacted party the opportunity to help create or to challenge a standard. It also provides an appeals process that contributes to legitimizing the entire procedure.

This dependence on consensus—as a community of interest—is a major strength but is also the single largest problem with which ANSI must deal. The problem, however, is part of the legacy of ANSI's creation. By refusing to seek governmental status, or even endorsement, ANSI placed itself in the position of having to depend on its ability to satisfy any legitimate organization that wanted to become a member. Initially, ANSI's clients were primarily engineers seeking a commonality in their technology and metrics. Over time, there was an increasing emphasis on the commonality of the parts, pieces, and materials that composed a physical system. Again, leadership was given to the groups or companies that received the greatest good from such standards—the capital-intensive manufacturing and utility companies. These companies long have been the leading proponents of standards, and, because of the magnitude and nature of their investments, they tend to move slowly, since a misadvised standard can be catastrophically expensive. However, the basic industrial makeup of the United States has been transformed over the past two decades: the industrial base is moving from capital-intensive, high-volume manufacturing to a service economy. This service economy, growing at a rapid rate, is predicated upon change and the encouragement of change, emphasizing adaptation to the current and future market, which seems transient to organizations that measure stability in decades. As long as the dominant force in the economy was the mainline manufacturing companies, hegemony in ANSI was theirs. Now, with the increasing economic power of the service and high-technology industries, this hegemony is no longer clear-cut. This conflict between the new, brash, high-change industries and the more stable older industries is one of the important challenges facing ANSI as a voluntary organization with no means to enforce its approach to standards except by consensus.

ANSI acts as the clearing house for voluntary standards from all major worldwide sources, including ISO, the IEC, and most of the most important national standards bodies. ANSI provides a centralized source of information on these standards for many export-minded companies—when they realize that non-U.S. standards must be implemented. While this observation may sound negative, it reflects an unfortunate and rather widespread phenomenon—major providers in the United States tend to produce for a domestic market. Many U.S. firms have never had to go outside of the country to sell their products. As a result, they do not understand that they must take national and international standards into account when they begin to design products and services for export. As the internationalization of trade and business accelerates and U.S. companies recognize that other countries have valid reasons for doing things their own way, demand for these standards will grow. Clearly, there must be a mechanism to disseminate information on international standards to ensure that U.S. companies are aware of international standardization activities— a standard serves no purpose if its existence is unknown. It is axiomatic that, if current publications were effective, these paragraphs on international standards would not have to be written.

Perhaps even more worrisome is the fact that not all U.S. companies are aware of what ANSI does. Of the several tens of thousands of U.S. companies, only about 1000 are members of ANSI. To gain a larger base of support, ANSI must promote understanding of its role in the standardization process, as well as the role of standards and standardization in general. This important task likely will be hindered by the ongoing conflict between mature/stable industries and young/ evolving industries, as well as by the lack of a single, unified position from all industry in the major councils. A broad base of active support will help the United States begin to understand the complexities of international standardization, but this base will take some time to build. I believe that the ultimate question is not whether ANSI will be able to create a better method for dispensing standards or cut standardization time from four to two years but rather whether the organization known as ANSI and the consensus standards method that it champions will survive the next decade.

ANSI: Membership and organization

The organization of ANSI, illustrated in Figure 12-1, resembles that of many other standards groups, such as ISO. However, it displays some unique characteristics, the result of the legislative branch's occasional investigations of structural problems in American industry and attempts to "fix" them. Because of this, ANSI has an apparent surfeit of checks and balances, which have served to make it a true consensus standards group.

ANSI's membership includes over 250 private industry and governmental organizations, and over 1000 companies. These diverse members are represented by the board of directors, which functions as ANSI's governing and policy-making body. The directors are drawn from many of the major industries and user groups that constitute the industrial strength of the United States; the board must ensure that equity is maintained among the members, and pains are taken to avoid overloading a single functional area on the board. Nominations are sought from the various interest groups, with limits on the number of directors who can be elected from a specific group, and are balloted by the general membership; other members serve *ex officio*, with several representing the federal government. The board provides general guidance to the activities of ANSI. In this duty, it is aided by the Executive and Finance Committees, which act for the board when it is not in session. These committees are charged with implementing the board's policy and overseeing ANSI's administrative function, as well as monitoring its financial well-being. In addition to the Executive/Finance Committees, several other subsidiary groups are of interest.

The Organizational Member Council and the Company Member Council are concerned with the organizations and companies that form part of the ANSI client base. Membership on these committees is open to any member of ANSI. Both groups act as conduits to and

Figure 12-1. Organizational structure of ANSI

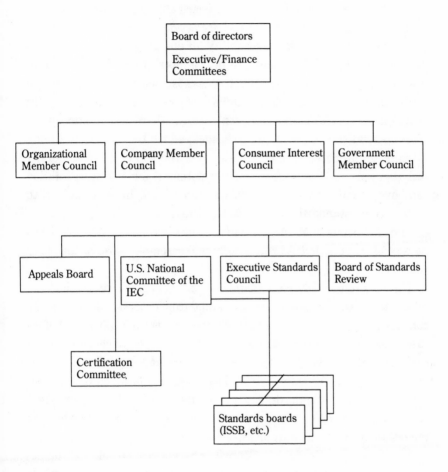

from the board of directors and the company and organization members. They are supposed to keep the board abreast of the latest areas of concern, inform it of occasions where action seems to be warranted, and, in turn, assume the responsibility for ensuring that the standards programs that ANSI pursues are in the interests of their members. For these committees, too, effectiveness is impacted by the lack of clarity in industry, the market, and society as a whole. Because there is no clear consensus in these committees, there is a tendency for them to send the board mixed messages, which the ANSI staff must attempt to interpret correctly to discover the will of the members. I feel that this lack of clarity and the potential for misinterpretation can, over time, erode the members' confidence in their ability to influence the standards process in the United States.

The Government Member Council is newly created. As yet, it has no official charter, but its goals likely will resemble those of the other councils.

The Consumer Interest Council is charged with protecting the interests of the consumer in the standards process. It represents consumers during standards development and is their advocate before the other standards boards. Its membership is open to consumers and their representatives, as well as to people and organizations with experience in the consumer field. The group can function either positively, affirming standards and proposing additional ones, or negatively, disavowing standards that will impose excessive burdens or unnecessary risks on consumers.

The Executive Standards Council (ESC) is responsible for the actual standards process—the activities of the standards makers. It manages the operating procedures, promotes expeditious completion of the standards activities, and generally acts as caretaker of the consensus process. Finally, this council is charged with coordinating U.S. participation in the technical work of international organizations.

The Certification Committee administers all of ANSI's accreditation activities for certification programs that other organizations wish to have accredited. Any certification program operated under ANSI accreditation must meet certain criteria. This committee helps to develop those criteria and recommends programs for acceptance as ANSI accredited programs. Additionally, it acts as a liaison with CASCO (Committee on Conformity Assessment), an ISO organization.

The Board of Standards Review sits in judgment on completed draft national standards. The concept of consensus is difficult, at best, to adjudicate, but it is the responsibility of this committee to see if consensus procedures have been followed, if disagreements have been handled properly, and if consensus has, in fact, been reached. Without this verification, either implicit or explicit, the power of the consensus process in the United States would be diminished, and the appellation of "American National Standard" would lose some of its meaning. It should be noted that, when they pass judgment on the concept of consensus, the members of the BSR serve as individuals rather than as representatives of a particular segment of ANSI.

The Appeals Board is the group within ANSI that responds to complaints that ANSI, through its action or inaction, has caused harm to a particular interest or faction.

The U.S. National Committee of the IEC is responsible for furnishing a U.S. national position on IEC matters to the Executive Standards Council. This committee confirms that U.S. participation in the work of the IEC is correct and timely and that the technical committees developing technical positions on IEC proposals function correctly.

Finally, eight Standards Boards report to the Executive Standards Council. Each of these boards advises the council on the management and coordination of the standards areas with which it is conversant. The Information Systems Standards Board (ISSB) is the group that advises the ESC on matters pertaining to information technology.

The day-to-day running of ANSI is the responsibility of the ANSI staff, headed by the president, who is appointed by and is responsible to the board of directors. Supporting the president is a staff composed of a general counsel, a Vice President of Communications, and five directors. These staff members have approximately one hundred other personnel working for them to see that standards are published and that the consensus procedure is followed, to develop new services, and to sell the standards of ANSI, ISO, and the IEC, as well as the national standards of over eighty other countries. Over 60 percent of ANSI's operating budget comes from the sale of printed standards, so the importance of this aspect of ANSI *to ANSI* should be apparent. It is also rapidly becoming a major area of contention between the stable, mature industries and the fast-changing and high-technology industries.

High-technology/high-change groups are more interested in the anticipatory information provided by the standards process than they are in the finished standards. The older, more stable industries, on the other hand, value the completed standard as a description of how things should be done for safety. As a result, the younger industries do not ascribe as much importance to ANSI's printed standards as the older industries do. To protect its revenue base, ANSI must satisfy the older industries, but it must also attempt to retain the support of the younger industries. As I mentioned earlier, I believe that this dichotomy and ANSI's ability to mitigate its impact will determine the future of ANSI in the United States.

ANSI: Procedures

All standards-developing organizations (SDOs) accredited by ANSI are voluntary bodies that operate under the concept of consensus, which, in turn, operates under "due process," a concept that provides anyone with a directly or materially affected interest in the proposed standard an opportunity to participate in its development, from its initiation through its completion. Consensus describes that point at which the developers and commentators of a standard merge in agreement; it should not be mistaken for majority or unanimity—consensus can be reached even when objections exist, as long as the developers believe that the objections are not significant enough to prevent the standard from being effective. While the procedure for reaching consensus is complex, it ensures that the standards produced by ANSI accredited groups meet the test of market need and acceptance.

The generalized process that must be followed is outlined below. Although it may vary somewhat depending on the standards group involved, it does give an idea of the checks and balances that are built into the system. In this description, the term "Accredited Standards Committee" (ASC) will be used to refer to Accredited Organizations and Accredited Canvass groups as well as ASCs. Thus, "ASC" refers to the three types of accredited standards-developing organizations. (For a more comprehensive discussion, see Chapter 8.)

A standard begins as a Project Proposal, which may be developed and submitted to an ASC by any individual. The proposal usually is reviewed within the ASC to determine if it fits within the mission of the ASC, as well as to review economic and functional validity. If the ASC believes that the proposal is valid, the full committee, or a representative portion, votes on it. If the vote is positive, the proposal is assigned to an appropriate ASC subcommittee, and the ASC Secretariat usually issues a press release soliciting technical contributions and membership. The subcommittee then develops a calendar and work plan and begins work on the proposal. When the draft proposed American National Standard (dpANS) is completed, the ASC community votes to determine if the document is ready for public review. The dpANS is also liable to review by an ASC subcommittee to verify that it complies with the approved proposal that started the development process. After the ASC review, the dpANS is ready to be forwarded for open public review.

The ASC Secretariat initiates public review of the dpANS. The ANSI publication *Standards Action* provides a brief description of the standard and announces that it is available for review and comment for the next four months. (It is during this phase that the concept of consensus comes into critical play.) Once consensus is reached, the full ASC votes on the proposal via letter ballot. The ASC Secretariat then forwards the proposal to the ANSI Board of Standards Review, which verifies that due process was observed and that consensus was, in fact, achieved. When the BSR is satisfied, the dpANS is approved and published as an American National Standard.

It should be noted that, in the actual process, multiple loops can occur, and multiple ballots can be much more complex to resolve than this outline suggests. However, even a bare-bones description reveals that the creation of an ANS is a complex process that involves all of the ASC and ANSI, with the technical experience of the ASC verifying that the standard is valid and suited to the industry, while ANSI ensures that all concerned individuals have the opportunity to examine and question the dpANS. It is this painstaking process that earns ANSI standards the high respect of both developers and users.

ASC X3: Accredited Standards Committee for Information Processing Systems

X3 is the Accredited Standards Committee for Information Processing Systems, operating under the procedures of the American National Standards Institute. X3 is one of the ANSI accredited committees under the purview of the ISSB, mentioned earlier. The Secretariat of X3 is sponsored by the Computer and Business Equipment Manufacturers Association (CBEMA).

A trade association that represents the information-processing, communications, and business products sector of industry, CBEMA, was founded as the National Association of Office Appliance Manufacturers in 1916 in Washington to act as the trade association of the business equipment industry. After several moves and name changes, it settled in Washington and became the Computer and Business Equipment Manufacturers Association. Membership in the association is open to all who engage in the engineering, manufacture, finance, sale, and support of all types of office equipment, computer systems and peripheral devices, telecommunications services, and business equipment. CBEMA operates in the interests of these members to provide the industry, as a whole, with a voice in the political and user arena. Its primary function is to provide an arena where companies identify and discuss issues of common concern. CBEMA has an additional goal of maintaining a degree of free and open competition in the industry, as well as sustaining and improving the public image of the information technology industry. CBEMA implements these goals in part through support of the ANSI approved voluntary consensus standards program.

CBEMA was asked to sponsor X3 when X3 first was proposed, and it agreed to serve as the Secretariat/sponsor of the committee and to accept responsibility for ensuring that the legal/financial/procedural requirements involved in the development of voluntary consensus standards under the ANSI procedures are met on those occasions when X3 cannot handle them on its own. This activity is not completely altruistic. Because ASC X3 operates under the procedures of ANSI, all interested parties must be involved in the standards process—that is, not only potentially all of the manufacturers but also all of the users and all of the governmental agencies that are materially and directly affected by the work of the ASC. The committee thus serves as a forum for the providers (whose organization CBEMA is) to explain their position while receiving valuable input from providers, users, government, and academia. It also permits anyone interested in information gathering to do so and encourages this type of activity.

X3 was formed in 1960, partially in response to the creation of TC 97 by ISO and the formation of ECMA. The following year, CBEMA accepted the Secretariat of the newly formed organization. After nearly a decade of rapid growth in the data-processing industry, X3 reorganized in 1969, establishing the technical committees that it now has. In 1980, the latest reorganization occurred; the X4 Committee (Office Machines and Supplies) was merged with X3, and X3 was given the charter for "standardization in the areas of computers and information processing and peripheral equipment, devices, and media related thereto; standardization of the functional characteristics of office machines, *particularly in those areas that influence the operators of such machines.*" The italics are mine, to highlight the significant emphasis that X3 places on designing standards that are useful to the ultimate user—the consumer. While all X3 standards require technical soundness, they also reflect the need and the will of the market. The adoption of an X3 standard occurs only after *all* concerned parties, including those who ultimately will cause acceptance or failure of the standard through their use or nonuse of it, have had an opportunity to review and comment on it. Once a standard is approved, X3 continues to provide interpretation and maintenance and makes certain that future standards do not conflict or do so only minimally.

X3: MEMBERSHIP AND ORGANIZATION. X3 is composed of forty-one members from the producer, consumer, and general-interest organizations in the information-processing industry. Membership must be balanced among these groups, so that no one group is dominant. Only organizations domiciled in the United States may participate, since X3 is the U.S. committee on information processing. The member organizations pay a service fee of between $3000 and $5000 per year to fund the Secretariat.

The simplified X3 organizational chart is shown in Figure 12-2. Each of the groups shown has its own distinct and clearly defined purpose; however, all share the larger common purpose of ensuring that the voluntary consensus standards procedure supports the information technology industry. Each level, beginning with ANSI, supports and interacts with the other levels so that compliance with the consensus process is assured and technically sound, economically usable standards are produced.

The X3 Secretariat manages over 500 projects and international responsibilities. It includes over seventy-five technical committees and their associated task groups, involving over 2500 volunteers. It maintains contacts with other standards organizations, manages the consensus requirements, provides guidance, interprets rules, and generally keeps everything running smoothly. All of these functions are carried out by nine staff members. The 1988 budget of X3 was approximately $600,000, generated by member fees and the sale of technical reports and X3 produced standards.

Three standing committees report to X3: the Standards Planning

Figure 12-2. Organizational structure of X3

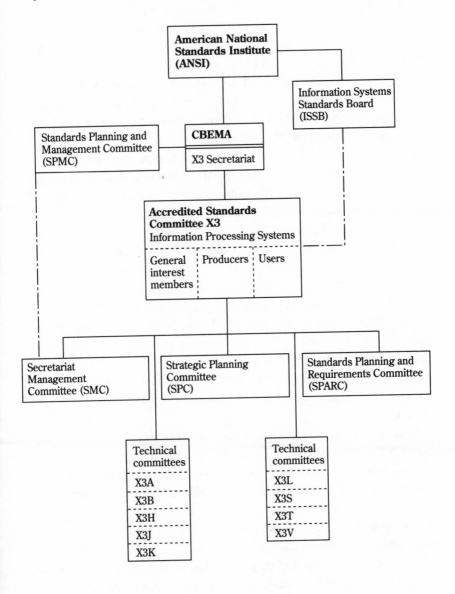

and Requirements Committee (SPARC), the Strategic Planning Committee (SPC), and the Secretariat Management Committee (SMC). SMC is an elected committee of nine people from X3 voting organizations. Its primary functions are to make sure that X3 subgroup officer positions are filled and that subgroup procedures are in compliance with X3 expectations; it also acts as an oversight committee for the X3 budgeting process. While the group is a standing committee of X3 and reports its activities to that organization, it has a dotted-line responsibility to the Standards Planning and Management Committee (SPMC), which is a CBEMA entity, reporting ultimately to the CBEMA board of directors. (SPMC's function is to formulate a CBEMA position on standards matters and to coordinate financial and administrative matters between X3 and CBEMA.)

SPC was established in 1988, and its formation reflects X3's acknowledgment that standards are becoming too complex to be dealt with on a case-by-case basis. As the Strategic Planning SWG serves JTC 1, SPC serves X3. Its function, however, is not confined merely to helping X3 manage the standardization process; SPC also has a responsibility to define the role of IT standards in the industry, to look at methods of improving the consensus process and at the rationale for some of the standards activities, and to coordinate activities so that X3 is not put in a position of playing catch-up in the international arena. Membership is open to anyone interested enough to participate.

SPARC, in which participation is limited to twenty people drawn from X3 dues-paying members, meets six times a year for three days. It has a wide range of functions, centered around the functional and economic aspects of standards. Part of this responsibility involves the evaluation of proposed standards projects to see how they fit within the scope of X3. This review ensures that few jurisdictional disputes occur among the SDOs that help create standards for IT and related industries. Once a decision on jurisdiction is made, SPARC helps to initiate the standards process by verifying that the objectives for the standard are valid—that is, that no potential technical solution is negated by the requirements and that the requirements reflect the need that the standard is projected to fill, both functionally and economically. Finally, SPARC acts as X3's project management team, monitoring and tracking the progress of the standard through the consensus standards process.

The work of X3—the development of standards for the IT industry—occurs in the technical committees (TCs). A technical committee is established by X3 to work only on projects within its assigned area of expertise. Membership in a TC is based on the single qualification that a member must be directly and materially affected by the activity and willing and able to participate actively. TCs, which are advisory to X3, produce draft proposed American National Standards (dpANS) and defend and interpret their work as necessary. Each TC has a chairperson, a vice chair, a secretary, an International Representative (the liaison with the appropriate ISO/IEC JTC 1 SCs), and a Vocabulary Representative (the liaison with TC X3K5, Information Processing Systems Vocabulary). (The details of the duties of these officers, along with the requirements for these positions, are all carefully defined by X3.)

There are seven main categories of technical committees, which cover the broad spectrum of the information technology industry. Each main subcommittee may have one or more subordinate committees assigned to it.

X3A Recognition
  X3A1 OCR and MICR

X3B Media
  X3B5 Digital Magnetic Tape
  X3B6 Instrumentation Tape
  X3B7 Magnetic Disks
  X3B8 Flexible Disk Cartridges

X3B9 Paper Forms/Layouts
X3B10 Credit/ID Cards
X3B11 Optical Digital Data Disks

X3H&J Languages
X3H2 Data Base
X3H3 Computer Graphics
X3H4 Information Resource and Dictionary
X3JI PL/1
X3J2 BASIC
X3J3 FORTRAN
X3J4 COBOL
X3J9 PASCAL
X3J10 APL
X3J11 C Language
X3J12 DIBOL
X3J13 COMMON LISP

X3K Documentation
X3K1 Computer Documentation
X3K5 Vocabulary for Information Processing Standards

X3L Data Representation
X3L2 Codes and Character Sets
X3L5 Labels and File Structure
X3L8 Data Representation

X3S Communication
X3S3 Data Communications

X3T&V Systems Technology
X3T1 Data Encryption
X3T2 Data Interchange
X3T5 Open Systems Interconnection

X3T9 I/O Interface
X3V1 Text: Office & Publishing Systems

X3: PROCEDURES. A standard begins as a Project Proposal, developed
and submitted to X3 by any individual. SPARC reviews the proposal
for its appropriateness to X3, as well as for economic and functional
justification. If SPARC approves the proposal, X3 as a whole votes
on it, and, if accepted, the proposal is assigned to a TC for development. At the same time, the X3 Secretariat issues a press release
soliciting technical contributions and members for the TC. Once the
TC is established, it develops a calendar and work plan. One of the
most important tasks of the TC is first to understand the purpose and
intent of the proposed standard and the technical issues that surround
it; only with this understanding can it get down to the work of writing
the standard. After the dpANS is completed, the X3 community votes
to determine whether the document is ready for public review, and
SPARC reviews it for compliance with the approved proposal. It is
then forwarded to ANSI for completion of the consensus process.

As an example of this complex and extremely time-consuming process, the last iteration of TC X3J4 (COBOL) involved the resolution
of over 3000 comments from the industry, users, and other impacted
parties. That this many comments were received testifies to the success of the concept of voluntary standards. Even more telling is that
all of the disparate groups managed to reach consensus on what this
version of COBOL should do and how it should do it. It took several
years and a substantial amount of work on the part of the committee,
but a standard that mirrored the needs of the users and producers
was created and is in wide use today.

Production of standards that are accepted and used is, in fact, what
makes X3 effective. The process is focused on creating a standard
that meets user needs and requirements; it is not meant to provide a
quick fix to a transient problem. Standards, as viewed by X3, are a
serious business, with serious economic and technical ramifications; to
treat them otherwise would be both careless and dangerous. The use

of volunteers and the enforcement of the concepts of consensus and due process, while not making for a quick turnaround, do provide very high quality, functional, and lasting standards.

U.S. Joint Technical Committee 1 Technical Advisory Group (U.S. JTC 1 TAG)

JTC 1 TAG is the newest standards group to appear on the U.S. IT standards scene. It is not an SDO but the replacement for the old X3 International Advisory Committee (IAC), which departed with the demise of TC 97 and the advent of the JTC 1. Because JTC 1 is an amalgam of ISO and IEC committees, it was felt necessary to create a U.S. committee that could represent all U.S. IT SDOs. IAC, as part of X3, could have continued as the international TAG to ANSI, but this was felt to be less than an optimal solution. As a result, a Technical Advisory Group (TAG) was created—not to write standards—but to provide a formal structure for the creation of U.S. positions on JTC 1 standards activities. ANSI assigned the Secretariat of this committee to CBEMA; as the organization that sponsors the Secretariat of the JTC 1 TAG, CBEMA has the same responsibilities as it has as the sponsor of the X3 Secretariat.

U.S. JTC 1 TAG: MEMBERSHIP AND ORGANIZATION. Figure 12-3 shows the current organization and composition of the JTC 1 TAG. Membership is open to members of X3 and any U.S. SDO impacted by IT standardization or wanting to participate in helping to advise ANSI on U.S. positions for the JTC 1. The group meets three times a year, usually but not always in conjunction with the X3 meeting. Because questions do not always arise at the convenience of the full TAG, a subcommittee has been formed to deal with the more pressing issues quickly. The JTC 1 TAG Advisory Committee (JT/AC) meets on a more frequent basis than the full TAG and acts for it in developing positions for the ANSI delegates to ISO.

As issues surface that impact more than a single U.S. IT SDO, the JTC 1 TAG creates special working groups (SWG) or study committees or uses other mechanisms to deal with these cross-organizational

Figure 12-3. Organizational structure of JTC 1 TAG

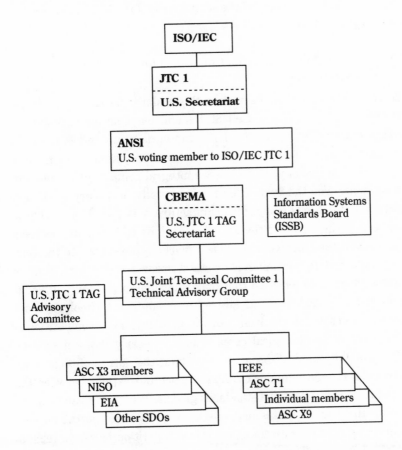

problems. At the same time, because it does act as the TAG for JTC 1, it must ensure that all of the activities in JTC 1 are mirrored, as necessary, in the U.S. activities.

ASC T1: Accredited Standards Committee for Telecommunications

One of the newer ASCs, T1 deals with standards for the telecommunications industry in the United States and plays an increasingly important part in the activities of IT standards programs. X3 and T1 are inextricably linked: telecommunications are essential to modern information technology, and IT is an integral component of telecommunications. Yet the two differ fundamentally on a very important point. Competition among IT manufacturers is based on technical advantage, which goes to the firm that exploits and manipulates technology the most quickly—change is a marketing weapon. In the telephony industry, the premium is on stable, proven technology, built on a tremendous installed base that makes change increasingly difficult. Backward compatibility and stable, problem-free technological advances are critical to the health of the industry, since competition is based, not on technological change, but on nearly flawless service. This basic philosophical disagreement about the nature of technology is, and will remain, a major stumbling block in relations between the IT and telecommunications standards groups. Whether it can be overcome in the United States depends in large measure on the success of the telephony operators engaging in competition based on technological advantage. The challenge internationally is much broader.

While many ASCs were created to help unify a market and champion a single standard set for an industry, T1 was formed in response to the disappearance of an industry's *de facto* standards maker, American Telephone and Telegraph. The dismemberment of that company produced a vacuum in the telephony industry within the United States—a vacuum that needed to be filled, and quickly. With the appearance of the "Baby Bells" and the growth of the telephone service companies, a reasonably stable environment was threatened with potential disaster. Although the restructuring of the industry promised to increase competition and therefore lessen the economic burden to the ultimate consumer, the disappearance of the unofficial standards-making body promised to make the industry disintegrate into a chaos of competing, noncomplementary products. In the information technology arena, this would be perceived as "goodness"; in the telecommunications industry, it would destroy the very basis of the market. It is this point that is critical to understanding T1: it serves a client base that wishes to standardize because the very survival of the industry depends on a standardized interconnect capability; there is no place in the public telephony network for a proprietary solution. If such a solution were to be offered, it would either fail because of lack of market acceptance, or it would succeed and destroy the remainder of the system.

To ensure that there was some centralized standards-setting body, on August 1, 1983, the industry formed the Exchange Carriers Standards Association (ECSA), with the twofold purpose of providing a public forum and representing exchange carrier interests in the standards process and the technology that fed these standards and of acting as Secretariat to a telecommunications ASC. Earlier, when the Federal Communications Commission had suggested that an existing regulatory committee be expanded to manage the standards process, both ECSA and ANSI had indicated that they felt that the private sector could manage the process more efficiently. As a result, when ECSA informed the FCC that it was prepared to support the Secretariat to a standards committee that would operate under the concept of ANSI consensus, the FCC welcomed the proposal. The call for participation in the ASC was announced in November 1983, and, in February 1984, T1 became the ASC for telecommunications within the United States, with ECSA acting as the legal and financial entity responsible for the Secretariat, much as CBEMA serves X3.

T1's primary function is to develop proposed American National

Standards that relate to the interfaces for the U.S. telecommunications system. (If standards describe how to interface to a system and what the system demands, the system itself, regardless of the provider, manufacturer, or user involved, will survive as a system, rather than decomposing into an assortment of ill-fitting parts.) T1 also monitors the activities of the CCITT and formulates positions that reflect the U.S. view on telephony interconnects, which it forwards to the U.S. CCITT national committee, run under the auspices of the State Department, and to the U.S. CCITT study groups, which are charged with representing the U.S. position to the State Department for presentation at the CCITT and the ITU. Finally, T1 produces reports that provide the industry's diverse constituents with an understanding of the potential directions and thoughts of the industry as a whole. The reports usually are produced by subcommittees, and their publication may or may not signal the imminent initiation of standards-writing activity.

T1: MEMBERSHIP AND ORGANIZATION. T1 presently has ninety voting members and seventy-five observers. Membership is open to any company, organization, individual, or government organization that has a direct and material interest in the activities of the committee. (This broad criterion for membership, which is shared by X3, is the key to the U.S. voluntary standards program, since it denies no one the opportunity to be heard.) Members fall into one of four interest categories: exchange carrier, interexchange and reseller, manufacturing and vendor, and users and general interest. Any group or individual belonging to one of these categories and meeting the other requirements for membership (attendance and payment of dues) is eligible to vote and hold office in T1. Other organizations may attend meetings but may not vote. To maintain balance in the organization, which is essential, T1 bylaws prohibit any one interest group from having sufficient representatives to form a majority, so that the diverse interests concept remains valid and no single group can monopolize T1 for its own interests.

Figure 12-4 shows T1's organizational diagram. The ECSA Stan-

Figure 12-4. Organizational structure of T1

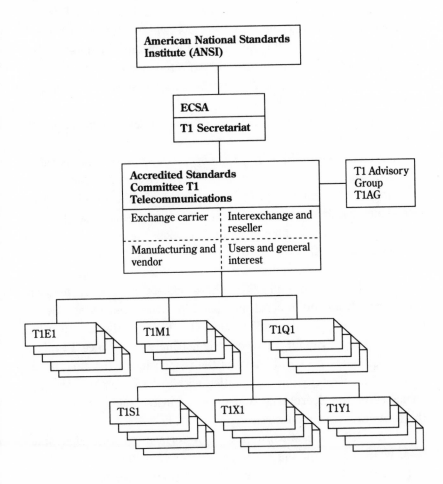

dards Advisory Committee (SAC) is responsible to ANSI for the sponsorship of T1, oversees the Secretariat, and monitors T1's conformance to ANSI procedures. ECSA has twenty-one directors on its board, over two hundred members, and a substantial budget to perform standardization and other industry functions for the telecommunications industry. (ECSA's membership represents over 95 percent of the telephone subscribers in the United States, which acts to legitimize its role in standardization for the telecommunications industry.)

The Secretariat of T1 is in charge of the day-to-day administrative duties that are vital to the committee. It is responsible for T1's organization and membership, for maintenance of T1's charter, and for compliance with the concept of consensus. It also supervises the creation of the standards for which T1 is responsible and ensures their publication by ANSI.

A chair, vice-chair, and two members of each interest group form the T1 Advisory Group (T1AG). These officers are elected for two-year terms from the general membership, nominated by the Secretariat and the general membership. The T1AG meets every other month and functions for T1 when it is not in session. Since T1 meets only three times a year, T1AG has the responsibility for most of the strategy and strategy implementation within T1. It monitors the performance of the Secretariat and provides instructions as needed to the technical subcommittees.

As with X3, the real work of T1 is performed in technical committees, which cover the entire range of interest of the four categories of participants. The six general technical committees and their subcommittees are:

T1E1 Carrier to Customer Installation Interfaces
   T1E1.1 Analog Interfaces
   T1E1.2 Digital Interfaces
   T1E1.3 Special Interfaces
   T1E1.4 ISDN

T1M1 Inter-network Operations, Administration, Maintenance, and
    Provisioning
    T1M1.1 Inter-network Planning and Engineering
    T1M1.2 Inter-network Operations
    T1M1.3 Testing and Operations Support Systems and Equipment
    T1M1.4 Administrative Systems

T1Q1 Performance
    T1Q1.1 4kHz Band
    T1Q1.2 4kHz Voiceband Data
    T1Q1.3 Digital Circuit
    T1Q1.4 Digital Packet
    T1Q1.5 Wideband Program
    T1Q1.6 Wideband Analog

T1S1 Services, Architectures, and Signaling
    T1S1.1 ISDN Architecture and Services
    T1S1.2 ISDN Switching and Signaling Protocols
    T1S1.3 Common Channel Switching
    T1S1.4 Individual Channel Switching

T1X1 Digital Hierarchical Structures and Synchronization
    T1X1.3 Digital Synchronization Interfaces
    T1X1.4 Metallic Hierarchical Interfaces
    T1X1.5 Optical Hierarchical Interfaces
    T1X1.6 Tributary Analysis

T1Y1 Specialized Subjects
    T1Y1.1 Specialized Voice and Audio Network
    T1Y1.2 Specialized Voice and Data Processing

T1Y1.3 Advanced Technologies and Services

T1Y1.4 Environmental Standards for Central Office Equipment

The divisions in the T1 committee structure show the emphasis on telephone interconnectability. However, T1E1.4, T1S1.1, and T1S1.2 are of special interest to the IT community because of their focus on the ISDN. Additionally, T1X1.5, Optical Hierarchical Interfaces, is concerned with fiber optics, mirroring some of the work in X3T9.

T1: PROCEDURES. The procedures of T1 for standards development are generally those of consensus that ANSI has promulgated. Because of the high interest and heavy participation in T1, as well as the legal controversy that caused T1's creation, the rules are followed very rigidly. Indeed, from the IT perspective, the search for consensus in the telecommunications industry at times seems to border upon the fanatic. This is, I believe, a carryover from the CCITT and the ITU, where consensus is interpreted as having all national states accept a position before the ratification of a piece of work can occur. As was noted earlier, consensus does not mean unanimity in the IT standards arena. This difference in the definition of consensus is another key element separating the IT and telecommunications standards worlds.

The Canadian Standards Association (CSA)

The Canadian Standards Association (CSA), in conjunction with the provincial and national governments of Canada, provides standards for regulatory purposes. It has no one counterpart in the United States; rather, it combines elements of the U.S. test houses, parts of the FCC, and some of the functions of ANSI. In close cooperation with the regulatory agencies, the CSA provides a single source for standards development, conformance testing, and regulations creation. The programs offered by the CSA are in support of Canadian industry, and the organization is dedicated to ensuring that the Canadian consumer is safe, assured of a quality product, and secure in the purchase of merchandise sold or made in Canada.

CSA: Membership and organization

Membership in the CSA is open to any Canadian citizen, business, or organization. The CSA is governed by its board of directors, elected every two years by the members of the association. The board manages the overall direction of the CSA; management of the day-to-day functioning is the responsibility of a board-appointed president, to whom report administrative functions for finance, administrative services, and human resources and an audit board. These groups, in effect, perform the functions of the Secretariat.

Three major administrative and functional divisions of the CSA also report directly to the president: the Standards Division, the Corporate Affairs group, and the Certification and Testing Division.

Corporate Affairs interfaces with the national and provincial governments and other organizations, provides marketing services, and acts as the CSA's primary link to the public. It also is charged with maintaining and increasing the membership of the CSA.

The Certification and Testing Division covers six major areas of testing and certification, ranging from communications equipment through anesthetic gas testing. It focuses on certifying that products and services meet the necessary Canadian or other national standards. The CSA assumes that most manufacturers have the necessary facilities to test their products before they submit them to the CSA for certification and approval; if they do not, the CSA will provide this service as well. Certification involves the submission of the product/service by the supplier, the verification of that product/capability by the CSA, and then continued follow-up audits by the CSA to ensure that the quality of the product/service is maintained. It should be noted that none of these services is free.

The CSA Standards Division operates under the concept of consensus to develop standards in eight broad areas: Lifestyles and the

Environment, Electrical/Electronics, Communications/Information, Construction, Energy, Transportation/Distribution, Materials Technology, and Production Management Systems. The managing body for the entire effort is the Standards Policy Board (SPB), the chair of which is responsible to the board, rather than to the president of the CSA. The SPB, composed entirely of volunteers, has the authority to establish Standards Steering Committees (SSCs), which are the managing committees of the eight areas in which standards are written. The SPB also sets policy on the writing of standards and monitors the activities of the SSCs.

Each SSC is responsible for the coordination of standards activities within its specific discipline and for the creation of the technical committees (TCs) that actually write the standards. The SSC names the chairpersons of the technical committees and attempts to balance the interests of the various groups in each TC to prevent undue influence by a single sector.

TC members are volunteers, drawn from consumers, manufacturers, government, labor, and consultants. Membership is based on expertise in the field and not, as in the United States, on significant or material interest. Members are required to pay dues, so a degree of commitment is necessary. There are now over nine hundred committees—some charged with only a single standard, and some having a wide range of responsibility. The TCs can create subcommittees to help in a particular aspect of a standard or to create a draft for consideration by the entire TC.

CSA Standards Division: Procedures

Standards development originates with a request from any of several quarters that is sent to the CSA for consideration. After a request is judged valid, it is sent for administration to the Standards Division, which then forwards it to the appropriate SSC for action. If the SSC determines that the request for a standard cannot be handled by an existing TC, it creates a new TC and appoints its officers. The committee then sets about acquiring members.

Writing a CSA standard involves several steps. A preliminary working draft is prepared within the TC and, after consensus is achieved within the TC, is rewritten (or possibly only retitled) as a committee draft. This draft is published as the work of the TC in the *CSA Information Update*, which elicits public comment. Comments received are evaluated, and the draft is changed (if necessary) to the CSA standard format and published as a CSA standard. This description oversimplifies the process, which is substantially more complicated in practice, with a series of checks and balances added to ensure consensus.

The CSA standards activities that are of interest to the IT community are the Electrical/Electronics program, which deals with the Canadian Electrical Codes and issues concerning performance of electrical products, and the Communications/Information program, which deals with telecommunications, computers, and office products, as well as electromagnetic interference. These two committees correspond to the EIA/UL (discussed in Chapter 13) and to X3, T1, and the FCC, respectively.

The boundary between regulation and consensus market standards is not as clear and distinct in Canada as it is in the United States. More of a crossover exists between voluntary and mandatory standards, partly because of the emphasis on protecting the public from itself and partly to ensure that the pace of technological change serves national interests—which is, after all, the ultimate rationale for any national standards body.

Deutsches Institut für Normung e.V. (DIN)

The Deutsches Institut für Normung e.V. (DIN) is the Federal Republic of Germany's national standards organization. Like the CSA, it has no single U.S. counterpart; although its functions include those that ANSI performs in the United States, DIN also carries out test and certification functions that are not handled by consensus standards organizations in the United States. Additional differences, unique to the nature of German business, will be discussed as part of this section.

The ultimate rationalization for DIN, and for DIN's importance in world standards, has been well stated in numerous articles by the organization's officers. Many of these articles repeatedly stress the importance of free trade, order in trade brought about by standardization, and the idea of free standards. Often, the texts praise the general concept of standards but will nearly always concentrate on the fact that their nation's GNP is heavily dependent upon foreign trade, which standards help to facilitate.

As was pointed out in the section on the CSA, the function of a national standards organization is to help the nation and its inhabitants. DIN works toward that goal in a manner similar to the CSA; however, it plays a more active role in the international standards arena to ensure that German products are being used and accepted internationally. Here, too, it is acting in the interests of the nation—in this case, by building the FRG's economic strength. Without this representation and awareness of the activities of national and international activities, German export capabilities might be severely impacted.

In an agreement between the government of the FRG and DIN signed in 1975, DIN was confirmed as the FRG's official representative at ISO, the IEC, and other national and international groups, including CEN and CENELEC. Approximately 15 percent of the ISO/IEC technical committees and subcommittees have DIN as a Secretariat, while in CEN/CENELEC, approximately 40 percent of the technical committees have a DIN Secretariat—an indication of the enormous significance that DIN attaches to participation in the international arena. The last two organizations are particularly important to DIN, since they serve as the basis for European standards, which are a key objective of DIN: the director of DIN, in a published statement, called for world trade free of technical barriers—and, in the next sentence, called for European standards for the European Common Market.

DIN has a reputation of having a very academic approach to standards. This reputation may be due to the heavy academic representation on DIN committees or to the fact that many DIN standards begin in academic research, which is then used to justify creating a standard for the industry.

DIN has several major principles, among them the voluntary nature of its work, a commitment to an open or public process, open participation, unity and precision, an international focus (within the constraints listed above), and a sensitivity to technical and economic issues. Finally, DIN has as a principle the good of standardization to the community as a whole: any standard must have a social value of benefit to the community. This raises an interesting issue of morality, at least as it relates to social utility—determination of a standard's "goodness," in anything other than general terms, would seem to present a major philosophical problem. Be that as it may, this is one of DIN's basic principles, and it must be considered when one looks at the standards that DIN produces.

As a consensus standards organization, DIN does not create regulations. As it points out, it has no machinery for imposing its recommendations upon anyone; rather, it relies on the technical excellence of its standards to win converts. However, DIN standards and the test houses that verify compliance to them have a unique position within the German business community: without the DIN testing and inspection mark, no insurance carrier in Germany will write insurance for a product. This constitutes a major business reason to accept and use DIN standards. Additionally, DIN standards serve as the basis for regulatory technical law in the FRG. While this is not uncommon in other countries, it is especially significant in the FRG—and, again, provides a business, as well as a legal, rationale, for using DIN standards.

DIN: Membership, organization, and procedures

Like other standards organizations, DIN's organization includes a central administrative group that manages the administrative and financial activities of DIN and the various committees that formulate the standards. These administrative functions cover the personnel, legal, financial, and publicity areas typical of any organization. There are also groups that focus on the publication of standards, the maintenance of the DIN test houses, and the entire process of testing. The administration is responsible to DIN's director, who is appointed by the president. The president is elected by the general membership, which consists of groups within Germany that have an interest in standards and includes representatives from the producers, the academic community, user groups and organizations (including consumer advocate groups), the government, and the trade unions.

As an indication of the size of DIN for purposes of comparison to other standards organizations, DIN e.V. has over five hundred and fifty employees, and nearly eight hundred full-time staff. (The difference between the two is that some DIN staff are not employed by DIN but rather are supported by their organizations or companies.) DIN has approximately forty offices in Germany, and 115 offices worldwide. There are over one hundred twenty major committees, with well over thirty-five hundred technical committees, composed of volunteers, that write the actual standards.

Completion of a standard is followed by a period of public comment and review. At the same time, DIN's Standards Examination Office reviews the document to verify that it does not conflict with other standards. Once a document has gone through the check-and-balance system, it is issued as a DIN standard in the body of German standards. At present, over twenty thousand DIN standards serve to standardize the German economy.

Association Française de Normalisation (AFNOR)

The Association Française de Normalisation (AFNOR) is the national public body in charge of standards for France. It publishes three types of standards documents: approved or mandatory standards, which must be used when the public market is concerned: experimental standards, which utilize new processes or techniques and are voluntary: and informational or guide standards. AFNOR's functions resemble DIN's, and it serves the French national interests in a manner similar to the other national standards bodies described in this chapter, although, in AFNOR's case, national interests are defined broadly to include the concept of political goodness as well as that of technical competence.

AFNOR was founded in 1926 as a private organization. The most recent modification to the organization's status occurred in 1984, when the framework of standardization in France was redirected. Standardization came to be regarded as a public service, and the private organization known as AFNOR was entrusted by the French government with certain responsibilities relating to standardization. These include sourcing, coordinating, approving, and promoting standards, training in the use of standardization, and controlling the use of the NF label—a trademark that shows compliance with a French national standard. AFNOR is also the French representative at international meetings. The program seems to be working, but its continued success appears to depend on the political attitude of the government.

AFNOR: Membership, organization, and procedures

A supraordinate body has been established to oversee the totality of the French national effort in standardization and standards: the High Council for Standardization, created in 1984, which is convened under the authority of the Minister for Industry and Research. This council is presided over by the chair of AFNOR, and its members include representatives from government, local communities, the various sectors of the economy (industrial, agricultural, service, and commercial), and unions, as well as standards participants, academicians, and scientists—fifty-one delegates in all. The council advises the Minister of Industry and Research on the direction that it believes standards will take and also comments on AFNOR's proposed general program.

AFNOR is governed by a board of directors, which is composed of senior civil servants appointed from the government ministries that are impacted most by standardization, members elected from the

AFNOR membership by the board for three-year terms, other generally elected members who serve as representatives with three-year terms, and experts appointed by the various ministries. The presence of civil servants indicates a concern that technology should not become an end in itself in the standards and that it serve the national interest as determined, not by the public, but by appointed representatives. The standards do not necessarily rise and fall on their own merit but rather on the merit of the ministry that supports their cause.

The board is charged with managing AFNOR and approving standards. To do so, it has established committees to deal with finances, consumer issues, international affairs, and certification. The committees usually are staffed by the board members but may, on occasion, be opened to outsiders.

There are two types of working groups in AFNOR—organization/follow-up and technical development/standards creation. Each of these groups has two separate and distinct functions. Within organization/follow-up, these are the Orientation and Follow-up Committees and the General Commissions. Neither of these does technical work; rather, they are responsible for the administrative management of the AFNOR standardization effort. The Orientation and Follow-up Committees initiate the standards work, defining the tasks at hand and assigning them to appropriate groups, which cover all areas in a single or related discipline and set up the process of standardization. General Commissions guide the standardization effort. Their tasks include national and international follow-up work, priority setting, and ensuring that each effort is carried out to its logical end.

Within the technical development/standards creation arena, there are two types of contributors—Standardization Committees and Expert Groups. Standardization Committees essentially are in charge of the technical standards creation that is done by the Expert Groups. The Standardization Committees establish the metrics, areas of technical competence, and activities of the Expert Groups, which are then convened to develop the standard. All Standardization Committees are identified with the suffix "CN" (for Comité Normalisation). When

"TI" also is appended, the committee is identified as working on matters relating to information technology. The numbering of the groups corresponds to the ISO JTC 1 numbering scheme. Expert Groups bear the identification "GE" (for Groupe Expert), and, they, too, are numbered based on their relation to the JTC 1 numerology.

The Japanese Industrial Standards Committee (JISC)

The Japanese Industrial Standards Committee (JISC), the national standards body of Japan, has no true parallel in other nations, since it seems to have a special relationship with the government and with the major manufacturers. Its organization resembles that of the other organizations in this chapter; however, its Secretariat is the Agency of Industrial Science and Technology, a division of the Ministry of International Trade and Industry (MITI). The publishing arm of the organization is the Japanese Standards Association, which publishes the standards that are developed under the auspices of JISC.

As the Japanese member body of the IEC and ISO, the JISC has come into its own as a force both in Japan and internationally in recent years, although it still lacks a certain degree of flexibility in its dealings with the rest of the standards community. The JISC exists primarily to ensure cooperation, not only between the various user industries and the IT industry, but also among the various major players in the IT arena. It must be remembered that standards have a very special and well-understood purpose in Japan—they are a marketing weapon, used to open or close a market. The goal of the JISC is to guarantee that Japanese industry can compete internationally in the IT and telecommunications industries.

One of the major functions of the JISC—a service provided to the IT industry as a whole—is monitoring. The JISC monitors the standards-developing activities of other national organizations—especially those of the United States—and can engage in bilateral and multilateral talks with these organizations. This is part of its stated goal of understanding the standards developments in the countries with which it competes and limiting foreign interventions into Japan. Where possible, the JISC bases Japan's national standards on international standards, with the result that the Japanese are able to implement and market an internationally standardized product very quickly.

The major Japanese organizations receive information on the activities of other national standards groups very rapidly because delegates report the results of their trips to their JISC committees. This contrasts with other nations, where standards delegates typically represent the interests of both their companies and their nation. In countries without a centralized planning structure, delegates will always come to the table with divided loyalties. If a delegate represents a company with multinational branches and no centralized planning structure exists for the country, the loyalties become very confused. The Japanese largely have avoided this problem because the JISC is under the Secretariat of MITI, which plays such a central role in Japanese industry. This makes gaining consensus on national standards issues less contentious. Having MITI as Secretariat also has strengthened the key areas of technical research and development concerning standardization. With MITI's influence and the willingness of major manufacturers to aid in the development of standards, the ability of the Japanese to capitalize upon a standard—and to implement it—is very high.

Foreign companies' involvement in the Japanese standards process is limited in many ways. Geographic and linguistic separation is a major obstacle, as are restrictions on the ability to obtain meaningful participation within JISC standards committees. Larger manufacturers can participate with a struggle, but user groups will find a mutual exchange very difficult; it is nearly impossible for small manufacturers to participate. The most effective dealings with some of the Japanese standards-developing organizations occurred during bilateral negotiations between governments.

The JISC's weakness is its limited ability to respond to the initiatives of the national and international standards bodies with which it deals. The very strength that the JISC gains from its association with MITI, and the strong consensus among manufacturers (and society as a whole) that this implies, gives rise to inflexibility in a rapidly evolving situation. Consensus requires that all impacted parties agree to one approach to a problem. Within Japan, and within MITI, this is done—each standard is assigned to a specific group that will develop it in conjunction with other Japanese manufacturers. This works well for reasonably straightforward product standards. But if the standard is a systems standard and if the draft standard is highly mutable, the possibility of internal consensus becomes far less likely. Within the older industries—such as steel, auto, and clothing—there is, as yet, little problem. Within the IT industry, however, the problems will become more and more critical.

Assume, for example, that the development of the layers of the OSI reference model has been assigned to various major Japanese companies to permit the Japanese IT industry to have a working model before anyone else. This strategy has proved highly successful in practice. It requires that the Japanese companies obtain internal consensus as to direction, scope, and technology and then begin to develop the model that they will use. Each company sees to its attendance at the necessary international standards meetings to drive the process, both internally and externally to Japan. The problem enters when a committee acts in a manner not foreseen by the Japanese. If, for instance, one of the layers is based on assumptions different from those with which the Japanese worked, and if these assumptions are standardized, the entire internal consensus concept is threatened. It may only need a minor repair, but, as the development proceeds, many minor repairs eventually will cause the larger vehicle to become inefficient and slow, if not stop it altogether.

Thus, the Japanese face a unique challenge. Unlike the other standards organizations, which suffer from a lack of planning, the JISC is threatened by its overreliance on planning and a belief that solutions can be managed completely. The IT standards world is populated by brilliant, iconoclastic individuals who will make their mark on standards; the consensus system in Japan has no mechanism to deal with these iconoclasts when they represent other nations and other concepts and act as change agents for the international IT industry.

The British Standards Institute (BSI)

The British Standards Institute (BSI) was created in the early 1900s, although it did not receive its present name and royal charter until the 1930s. The BSI is the official British representative to ISO and other national and regional standards bodies and deals with the PTTs. The organization is charged with coordinating all standardization efforts in the United Kingdom to ensure simplification of production and distribution of goods and services, thereby eliminating the waste of both time and material that is occasioned by duplication; to set up and promote standards for quality and dimensions for manufacturers and other parties; and to certify those products that comply with BSI standards. The ultimate function of the BSI, however, is to protect the British citizen from shoddy goods and services. The BSI is doing this, in concert with ISO, in its standards activities. Where possible, it adopts an ISO standard for use in the United Kingdom. When it can, it promotes BSI standards for adoption internationally.

The BSI is a voluntary organization, with membership open to interested parties ranging from nationalized industries all the way to professionals and consulting engineers. Like DIN, the organization is funded by its members, the government, and revenues from the sale of standards. The work of standardization is done by technical committees, which follow the same process methodology as the other national standards organizations.

A major distinction of the BSI is the existence of the Hemel Hempstead Division, a test house owned and operated by the BSI. The Hemel Hempstead test house administers the BSI Quality Assurance Program; the BSI then provides a compliance mark to any product or service that meets the requisite standards for British quality.

13. GOVERNMENTAL AND
USER STANDARDS BODIES

The glories of our blood and state
Are shadows, not substantial things.

The Glories of Our Blood and State
James Shirley

Two distinct types of standards bodies traditionally participate in the consensus standards process. Voluntary user groups caused the formation of the present consensus standards groups throughout the world; they were helped, in most instances, by the activities of governmental organizations.

Voluntary organizations are, usually, associations of like-minded individuals who have gathered together with the avowed purpose of furthering their discipline and maintaining the professionalism that the discipline fostered. These organizations—or societies or unions— define the limits of professionalism, give credence to a larger idea of professional discipline and accountability, and generally are interested in creating and maintaining the standards that they believe exist within and for their profession.

The government, on the other hand, is involved in areas that affect the public good. To promote the common good and, where it may be threatened, to ensure that the common good is protected, governments have established their own standards organizations.

Professional associations tend to be led by the last generation, since leadership is often a function of age and experience, and governments usually respond rather than initiate. The belief that the past should serve as a guide to the future and that evolution, not revolution, is important is the hallmark of both of these groups. Just as national standards bodies work to protect the national interest (since the nation is their client), associations and governmental standards groups seek to protect their clients—the group that makes up the association and the bureaucracy of the governmental agency.

Both types of organizations can function extremely well in a relatively static environment; however, the most significant feature of the IT industry is the rapid rate of technological change—technology is now a competitive weapon in the quest for market share. The two groups, which are structured to permit and encourage gradual, proven change with a minimal impact on their client groups, cannot keep pace with IT, where professional life spans are approximately seven years, unless professionals continuously update the technical base on which their education is built. Experience has been devalued in favor of education—all the experience in the world in transistors will not help someone understand layer five of OSI.

In many situations, however, promotion is based, not on technical or managerial competence, but on seniority, a form of experience. This places associations in an interesting position in the IT community: are their managements elected because of technical competence, because of managerial competence, or because of seniority? Within a corporation, this question is less important, since it is expected that a person with a technical ability either will be educated further or will learn the discipline of management. Within a society devoted to professionalism in a discipline, it is expertise in that discipline that counts, and, most often, it is the younger engineers—who have the advantage of a more current education—who are the most technically competent and, by implication, the most professional in the discipline.

Within the governmental standards arena, the lure of the higher salaries available in academia, let alone in industry, has been effective in removing a large amount of expertise. Those that remain usually are dedicated professionals who help to create standards because they are an expression of how things should work, rather than treating standards as a pragmatic vehicle to achieve a business purpose. Governmental groups also have the potential for leadership, since they can convince diverse interest groups to work together for a common good—even though their activities are not always appreciated by users and producers, they usually act in good faith.

In both areas—society and government—there has been a shift away from the older style of standards activity. Both groups have sought ways to influence the activities of the leading national SDOs, and both have achieved some successes, as well as some failures. Additionally, user groups have mutated into a new form of computer standards group made up of users and producers representing special interests. Companies, users, and representatives of government now band together to press for the adoption—either *de facto* or *de jure*— of a single standard in which they have a significant interest. There is no attempt at equal representation—these are not free organizations. Participation involves a membership fee, and members provide the participants who work on the standards issues.

User organizations

The Institute of Electrical and
Electronics Engineers, Inc. (IEEE)

The Institute of Electrical and Electronics Engineers (IEEE), one of the largest professional organizations in the world, has as a fundamental goal the advancement of the theory and practice of electrical and electronics engineering. Members are admitted upon the recommendation of a current member and are required to pay dues to the organization. There are other criteria for entrance, primarily, that the member must be technically qualified in an electrical/electronics, computer, communications, or associated technical discipline. The organization is broken into societies—distinct and identifiable groups representing either a technical discipline or an industry. The societies are equal but separate, and each has its own structure and form.

The IEEE's general membership elects the twenty-four members of its Assembly, which must meet once a year. The members also vote for the president and some of the other officers; the Assembly appoints the remainder of the officers. The Assembly then becomes the board of directors, with the addition of eight more members, voted in by the Assembly. A subset of the board becomes the Executive Committee, responsible to the board and acting for it between meetings. The Executive Committee appoints the General Manager, who is responsible for the day-to-day operation of the IEEE.

Eight major boards within the IEEE report to the board of directors. These range from the Technical Activities Board, which is composed of all of the IEEE societies and councils, to the Conference Board, which is charged with helping to arrange conferences and conventions. The Standards Board is the ultimate IEEE authority on matters relating to standards. The chairperson of the Standards Board is elected by the Assembly and holds the title of Director, Standards Activities. The Standards Board itself consists of between eighteen and twenty-four members, who vote on proposed IEEE standards. (See Figure 13-1.)

IEEE standards usually are written in the society with a dominant interest in the area. A society that wants a standard created must first agree to sponsor the standard and then must submit a Project Authorization Request (PAR) to the New Standards Committee (NesCom), which examines it for completeness and applicability by/ to the IEEE and verifies that the proper organization in the IEEE is acting. If it approves, the NesCom then forwards the request to the Standards Board. If the Standards Board approves the PAR, the society responsible for creation of the standard is charged with compiling an interest list of possible members, coordinating the activities of the standards committee within the IEEE, and generally ensuring that the concept of consensus, as required by ANSI rules, is followed. When the standard has been completed, it returns to the Standards Board through the Standards Review Committee (RevCom) for final review, approval, and publication as an IEEE standard.

Because the IEEE is recognized as an Accredited Organization, it *may* submit its standards directly to the ANSI Board of Standards

Figure 13-1. Organizational structure of the IEEE

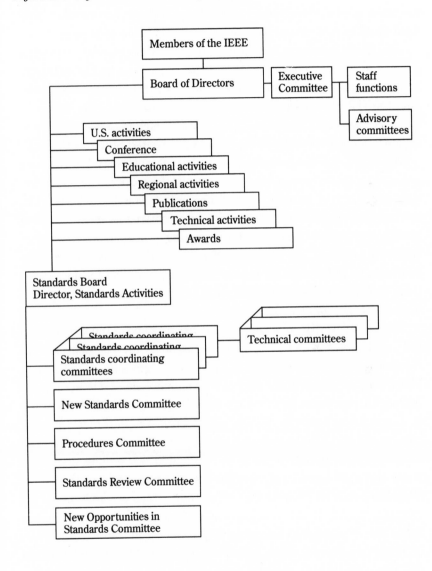

Review for adoption as American National Standards. Again, consensus must be observed, and all parties impacted by the proposed standard must have a chance to vote on it as it is being processed.

The IEEE's standards deal primarily with devices; there is little activity in the systems arena, where the majority of highly influential standards work should occur in the next several years. Internationally, the IEEE tends to concentrate on the Executive Committee of the U.S. National Committee (U.S.N.C.), which is part of the ANSI organizational structure and represents the United States at the IEC.

The IEEE standards manual notes that international standards are primarily a tool of commerce and, as such, the work of these committees is mainly of interest to manufacturers. The IEEE's interest, however, is not so much in the area of commerce as in the areas of terminology, safety, and "good engineering practice," a phrase that occurs throughout the IEEE's references to standards work. The emphasis in IEEE standards is on the validity of the technical solution, rather than the practicality of the standard as a solution to a business or economic need.

This technical discipline and focus constitute one of the strengths of the IEEE, as well as one of its major weaknesses. The penchant for pioneering new fields of technology has paid handsome dividends at times and, at other times, has led to nonimplementable standards. Among the successes is the work done by the IEEE 802 Committee on Local Area Networks (LANs). This work was in the van of technology, and it created a new industry. The IEEE had undertaken the standardization project because no other SDO was willing to do so—there appeared to be no market for the standard. Indeed, the IEEE often has taken on projects that other committees wouldn't touch; for example, IEEE 1003's development of the POSIX standard, which led to the creation of yet another major market in the IT industry.

These achievements are balanced, however, by numerous forays into areas that are technically sound but of little use to the IT community. No major IT vendor was able to implement IEEE P854, a radix-free floating point standard, and P854 superseded P754, which had equal or greater deficiencies. Other standards being developed duplicate and overlap current or planned activities. These proposals, which are initiated based on their technical merit, differ from one another on arcane technical points. The consideration of "what problem?" is lacking; instead, the question is "what solution?" and this usually results in a discrete solution to a single current problem. Moreover, the IEEE tends to establish umbrella organizations that attempt to include as much technical territory as possible under the umbrella, and the standards produced are point projects. What coordination exists is provided by the parent society responsible for that particular standards activity.

The Computer Society of the IEEE is the primary producer of IEEE standards for the IT industry, as opposed to the electrical engineering industry. It became active in the creation of standards in 1980 and has published standards in areas as diverse as 32-bit backplane, FORTH, and the Software Life Cycle Process. By mid-1987, it had published thirty-six standards and had eighty-two active working groups. Currently, the Computer Society is the fastest growing area of standards activity in the IEEE.

The IEEE, as a whole, continues to stress product standards for safety, measurement, and so on, which are still necessary and sought after by the component segment of the IT industry. Standards dealing with the concept of the "systemness" of a computer are less well developed, because of the bias in favor of technical, rather than economic, solutions. It is this problem that the Computer Society will have to address: understanding what industry, or industry segment, it serves. If the Computer Society wishes to serve the component side of the computer industry, it should focus standardization efforts there; if it wishes to serve the larger, system-driven portion of the industry, it must modify its perception of what a computer standard is.

The IEEE, as a professional society, serves its members. The question is whether its members should see themselves as engineers first and members of a company or industry second, or whether they should put their membership in an economic organization ahead of their membership in the IEEE. At this time, the IEEE believes that being an engineer is more important than being a member of a company, academic community, government, or other organization. This assumption—and the IEEE's assumption about standards—will be tested over the next decade.

The Electronic Industries Association (EIA)

The Electronic Industries Association (EIA), another Accredited Organization operating under ANSI's rules of consensus, is a trade organization representing a large number of manufacturers in the United States, from whom dues are required, based on sales. The EIA was founded in 1924 as the Radio Manufacturers Association and has grown substantially since then. In 1988, it had over two hundred twenty standards committees with over four thousand representatives from industry and the government. Currently, its standards, position papers, and publications exceed four hundred.

Standards work is done under the aegis of the EIA Engineering Department, which reports to the president of the EIA. (See Figure 13-2.) Five other major interest groups also report to the president; of these, the EIA Information and Telecommunications Technology Group (ITTG) is the most relevant to this book.

When one of the ITTG's four divisions (Fiber Optics, Mobile Communications, Network Equipment, and User Premises Equipment) believes that a standard is necessary, it advises the ITTG Technical Council, which then works with the Engineering Department to create the standard. In effect, the Engineering Department fills the roles of the IEEE Standards Board and the IEEE societies in monitoring the activities of the standards as they progress through the consensus process.

The standards are developed in technical committees, which can form subcommittees to work on specific areas of the standards. Technical committees report to the ITTG Technical Council, and thence to the Engineering Department. As with IEEE, EIA standards are

Figure 13-2. Organizational structure of the EIA

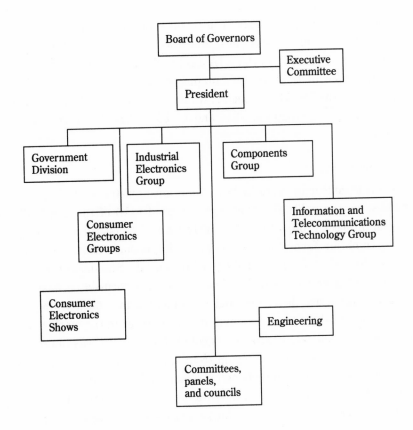

forwarded to ANSI for review when it is felt that they should become American National Standards.

The EIA's standards work focuses on connectors, wiring schema, residential consumer electronics, and low-level physical interconnections, areas of concern to the EIA's clientele, the manufacturers and users of much of this type of equipment. The best known of their standards is the RS-232 connector, which every person who has looked at a computer terminal has seen and probably has had to connect or disconnect.

Standards consortia

Standards consortia seem to have come into existence for the same purpose as the political action committees (PACs) of the mid-1970s, special-interest groups that effectively lobbied legislatures and legislators to obtain favorable laws by gathering enough constituents and enough financial backing to make their power felt. Standards consortia usually are user and provider driven; they are focused on ensuring that standards are developed and implemented in a fashion that fits the special needs of their members (the remainder of the market will, they believe, follow). The original goal of these groups was to provide users and providers with a forum from which to influence standards; the intent now seems to be to tell the market how to "do standards." Since 1985, the voices of the consortia have become increasingly shrill as they attempt to compensate for lack of material progress by promising more.

The Manufacturing Automation Protocol (MAP), the Technical Office Protocol (TOP), and the Corporation for Open Systems (COS) represent the first generation of standards consortia.

MAP is a manufacturing protocol initially designed by General Motors Corporation, which advocated this protocol for use in manufacturing automation when it began to automate its factories. The standard did not cover all of the automotive industry, not was it specific to that industry; rather, it was intended to provide a backbone to which everything else could attach, thereby assuring the stability and rigidity of the structure as a whole. The problem with this approach, however, lay in the correct specification of the proposed standard and the organization of the standards committee. Much of the work was done in expectation of an immediate payback—and few standards produce such a quick return. Additionally, I do not feel that the developers of the MAP standard were willing to devote the time required to develop an IT standard that would work well, broadly, and over the long run. Impatience in developing IT standards, especially in dealing with the constant change in technology, is typical of many firms, especially those accustomed to a structured and stable environment.

TOP is in the same class. It was initiated by Boeing as a response to the perceived lack of activity by the voluntary standards communities to develop a LAN specifically aimed at a technical office environment. TOP has gained some adherents, but, once again, the majority of users have been slow to accept it, primarily because the environment and potential application of LANs are changing so rapidly.

In both of these cases, members of the organizations established a solution to a specific problem by freezing a technology, and, in both cases, technical developments appear to have overtaken the technologies fixed in the early standards. This has resulted in constant revisions and conflictive reports from the committees and participants, which have the potential for splintering activities. The question becomes whether or not an organization can expand its role while maintaining its original focus on creating a tailored standard.

Finally, there is COS, an industry group funded by parties interested in participating in Open Systems Interconnect. OSI is being developed in ISO/IEC JTC 1, and nearly every national organization is participating in the effort. The original purpose of COS was to rally support for the standard by promoting the use of OSI standards. Ultimately, however, COS moved into the certification and conformance testing arena, creating test suites intended to validate whether or not providers' offerings meet International Standardized Profiles;

if a product/service passed the appropriate test suite, it would receive a "COS mark." But OSI itself is not yet stable, because of the complexity of the concept and the enormity of the standards effort, and, without a stable standard, stable test suites cannot be developed. Again, the assumption was that, once a standard is written, it freezes technology. In the IT industry, this is untrue.

Other consortia have also appeared. All seem to have arisen from a belief that, by claiming the right to represent a special segment of the industry, they have the right to decide what will (and, by implication, what will not) be a standard. Their common feature is a conviction that they alone know the the truth and that they alone are the arbitrators of what should happen in standards.

However, as the consortia age, they are finding that standards are difficult to create and to maintain, in need of constant care and attention. Moreover, standards are the exception in the United States, where the ethic emphasizes competition—which, in the IT industry, is based on technological innovation and fierce independence. When standards are given heavy publicity and expected to perform immediately, they have a high mortality rate, as do the organizations that have touted them as the cure for the problems of the industry. Any participant in standards must understand and accept the difficulty of the act of creation and try not to force it. This is the lesson that the consortia are in the process of learning—sometimes painfully.

Governmental organizations

The Department of State

The Department of State is the government entity responsible for voicing and voting the U.S. position on matters of the ITU, which, as a U.N. treaty organization, requires representation by national governments because they can commit to international treaty obligations. To carry out this task, the State Department relies on the expertise of a committee called the United States Organization for the International Telegraph and Telephone Consultative Committee (the U.S. CCITT). This committee is headed by the Office of International Communications Policy, which is part of the Bureau of Economic and Business Affairs. The National Committee is the management group responsible for the effective functioning of the U.S. CCITT, including the administrative and nontechnical aspects of its study groups.

Since national contributions form the basis of the work of the CCITT, and hence the ITU, it is vital for U.S. interests to have adequate representation. To assure that all voices are heard, the U.S. CCITT is open to all interested parties—from dues-paying members of the CCITT to users, manufacturers, national standards organizations, and the governmental organizations interested in this area. The U.S. CCITT operates in study groups, and an organization requests membership from the chair of the appropriate study group, not from the Department of State.

The study groups are responsible for their technical work, which consists primarily of reviewing the contributions that the U.S. CCITT will forward to the CCITT to influence or to provide a basis for its recommendations to the ITU. These contributions, which the ITU will call "U.S. Contributions," fall into two categories: contributions by CCITT members—called individual-member contributions—and contributions by non-CCITT members.

The U.S. CCITT also serves as a pool from which skilled personnel are drawn to represent the United States at the CCITT Plenary Assembly, which is held once every four years. These people are also available to the United States as delegates to working group meetings or to represent the United States at other CCITT meetings.

The United States has adopted this system because of the nature of its telecommunications industry, a private-sector activity that has grown substantially since the breakup of AT&T. The U.S. CCITT is structured so that all companies with an interest in the telecommunications market can participate in the committee's activities, whether or not they are members of the CCITT. Other national governments do not have to accommodate this degree of private-sector interest and instead use governmentally sanctioned Postal, Telegraph, and Telephone (PTTs) administrations in their dealings with the CCITT.

The National Institute for Standards and Technology (NIST)

The National Institute for Standards and Technology (NIST) is the new name of the organization known until recently as the National Bureau of Standards (NBS), which was created by an act of Congress in 1901. The name change occurred in 1988, following passage of the Omnibus Trade and Competitiveness Act of 1988. NIST will assume all of the functions of the NBS, along with several new functions, including helping to ensure that technology transfer occurs, that small business can use this technology, and that technological competitiveness is retained. Funding has not increased substantially.

NIST is the most important of the government organizations involved in standardization. Its function is to help remove barriers to trade and new technologies, as well as to provide a national laboratory for use by academic, business, and governmental interests. Its major rationale lies not in its standards activities, per se, but rather in its ability to help the academic, private, and governmental sectors better utilize technology and technological advances.

Much of the standards activity by NIST is in the voluntary consensus standards area, where NIST personnel attend standards meetings and act to disperse their findings to this arena. A great deal of the effort is aimed at non-IT activities, since NIST serves the entire U.S. effort, as ANSI does. However, one section of NIST does specialize in IT matters: the National Computer Systems Laboratory (NCSL), formerly the Institute for Computer Sciences and Technology (ICST), formed in 1966 in response to the Brooks Act of 1965. The Brooks Act was essentially a procurement act to resolve the problem of incompatibility in computer systems within the federal government, an issue complicated by the fact that there were no clear specifications on what to buy. With the Brooks Act, the federal government was given a mandate to standardize its procurement practices.

To meet this mandate, the NCSL (ICST) developed Federal Information Processing Standards (FIPS), federal government procurement standards quoted in procurements for ADP equipment for the government. Over one hundred fifty FIPS are currently in effect, covering everything from languages to peripheral interfaces. The ultimate purpose of the FIPS is to decrease the cost to the government of computers, both in terms of procurement and of the manpower used to operate them.

NCSL has understood that a federal standard is largely useless if it is not backed by the IT industry and users. Simply mandating federal standards would be counterproductive and would not serve the government, the user, or the producer. With this realization, the NCSL encourages its employees to participate in the IT industry's standardization process. Because of their high degree of technical expertise, NCSL members are welcome at SDO meetings, where they often can provide information about developments in the NIST laboratories, as well as gathering industry information for consideration by the government.

The NCSL is largely out of the standards-creating business now. As more and more standards were developed by the consensus process, NCSL recommended adding them to the list of FIPS, rather than creating new standards. However, when the government needs a standard, and the industry and its standards groups do not respond to this need, the NCSL has the ability to develop its own FIPS—a procedure that it normally avoids but has the technical competence to achieve. Because it always has this option, and because the government is the largest single purchaser of IT equipment in the world, the NCSL sits in a position of influence. But this position is precarious: if the NCSL chooses to use its power to create a standard, its influence may be diminished by the ensuing political backlash; if it chooses not to exercise its authority as the government's standards maker even though a standard clearly is needed, it risks losing the goodwill of its client—the U.S. government. The NCSL walks a narrow and dangerous path, buffeted by all sorts of pressures. So far, it has not lost its footing.

The General Services Administration (GSA)

The General Services Administration (GSA) was established under the Federal Property and Administrative Services Act of 1949, in which the GSA was authorized to prescribe standard purchase specifications and to direct their use in the governmental procurement process. To carry out this charge, the GSA developed the Federal Standardization Program, which covered all product standardization efforts in the federal government. The GSA normally delegated developmental responsibility to another agency but retained the authority to approve and implement its standards for the government. The GSA acknowledged the Office of Management and Budget Circular A-119, which establishes the primacy of the national consensus standards method as a source for standards.

In 1965, the Brooks Act transferred the responsibility for ADP standards development from the Federal Standardization Program to the NBS/ICST (now NIST/NCSL), and, in 1972, development of telecommunications standards was moved to the National Communication System, a branch of the Department of Defense. (A 1987 amendment to the Brooks Act redefined certain standards as ADP, rather than telecommunications, which moved them to the NBS [NIST], where they presently reside under the FIPS program.) The GSA, however, retains implementation authority for these standards under the authority of the Federal Information Resources Management Relations (FIRMR).

Since its creation in 1949, the GSA has seen two major areas of standards development removed from its control—the two areas that experience the highest level of change and the greatest need for technological expertise. However, because it has a substantial voice in determining procurement methodologies and because it is viewed as the caretaker of the governmental standards effort, the role of GSA as the ultimate arbitrator of implementation standards should not go unnoticed. The GSA has the final authority in one of the most important areas of governmental programs for standardization—deciding who can sell/buy what to/from whom. It is the economic aspect of a standard that makes it valuable, and it is this aspect over which the GSA exerts power.

14. COMPLEMENTARY

STANDARDS BODIES

> And post o'er land and ocean without rest;
> They also serve who only stand and wait.
>
> *On His Blindness*
> John Milton

The organizations examined in this chapter are not true IT standards bodies in that IT is not their primary focus, but they all have some relation to the primary IT SDOs. Because they are not among the main IT SDOs, which are the concern of this book, only a thumbnail sketch of each is offered, listing some of the projects with which each is involved and the potential impact that these projects can/could/ should have on the major IT SDOs.

ASC X12: Accredited Standards Committee for Electronic Data Interchange

ASC X12 is the committee formed to create, develop, and maintain standards for the electronic data interchange (EDI) of business transactions. Chartered in 1979, it based its original development on the work of the Transportation Data Coordinating Committee. Using the extant base, X12 has developed standards for electronic interchange of purchase orders and invoices, as well as payment advice transaction standards, activities that traditionally fall under the general category of "business transactions." However, the term has taken on increased significance in the past several years, as more and more firms have gained on-line, interactive computing capabilities and wish to expedite processes that involve a great deal of manual paperwork; it eventually may come to cover all aspects of a contract, not merely the invoice and payment portions.

As an ANSI ASC, the organization is open to all interested or materially affected parties. X12 has four subcommittees reporting to its chairperson: X12A (New Transaction Development), X12B (Maintenance, Liaison, and Data Dictionary), X12C (Communication and Controls), and X12D (Education, Implementation Aids, and Public Relations). The Secretariat for X12 is held by Data Interchange Standards Association, Inc.

X12 is of interest to the IT community because the basis of electronic data interchange is IT equipment. As X12 has been developing its standards from the application side, X3 and JTC 1 have been developing theirs from the provider side. Unfortunately, instead of meeting on common ground (probably in the OSI arena), the groups have tended to ignore one another and are developing similar, but incompatible, standards, especially in the areas of OSI. This finally is being addressed by the various standards committees; still, the lack of a clear definition of the term "EDI," as well as its implications, leaves large opportunities for potential and actual overlap.

The Human Factors Society (HFS)

The Human Factors Society (HFS) is the ANSI Accredited Organization for development of standards relating to ergonomics. Among its responsibilities are ergonomic standards for IT equipment, including ergonomic design of computer hardware and computer software.

The HFS is the ANSI TAG for ISO TC 159, the ISO technical committee for ergonomics. TC 159 looks at the designs and concepts that underlie the ergonomic designs of all products and not merely those of the IT industry. However, the portion of its work that does touch the IT industry is very influential, as it forms the basis for product design and concomitant legislation in several European and

Asian countries. The standards produced by TC 159 also are beginning to be required by law in the United States.

The HFS has a high level of international credibility in the standards arena and is heavily involved in the creation of international standards, as well as in the basic research that supports those standards. Because the work of the HFS and its international equivalent TC 159 has a distinct impact on the IT market, it should be more fully understood, appreciated, and participated in by the IT industry.

ASC Z39: The National Information Standards Organization (NISO)

ASC Z39, run under the auspices of the National Institute for Sciences and Technology (NIST), focuses on library, information science, and publishing standards. However, as IT becomes increasingly important to the profession of library science, Z39 has become more active in the creation of IT standards serving information sciences and publication management. And, as the IT industry became more involved with information science concepts and electronic publishing, it became aware that an organization already was writing standards for these areas. At first, each group occasionally would propose standards that were incompatible with those published by the other group, but the cooperative liaison between IT participants and NISO has been growing. ASC Z39 now uses parts of ISO JTC 1 standards where necessary to complement its current standards activities.

NISO currently has twenty-three standards committees working on draft standards. The standards cover a broad range of topics, from Z39.21-1980, Book Numbering, to Z39.58-198x, Common Command Language. Several new work items concern topics in the realm of desktop/electronic publishing and information storage and retrieval, areas of high interest in the IT community.

NISO is the U.S. representative to ISO TC 46, Information and Documentation, which is concerned with the the standardization of practices relating to libraries, documentation and information centers, indexing and abstracting services, archives, information science, and publishing. An obvious opportunity for coordination with the IT industry exists in TC 46/SC 4, Computer Applications, which looks at the standardization of methods and procedures for the use of computers in information and documentation, including communication protocols and formats, character sets, command language, and data element directories.

The Instrument Society of America (ISA)

The Instrument Society of America (ISA) is an ANSI Accredited Organization concerned with developing standards in the area of instrumentation and control. Additionally, it holds the Administrative Secretariat for the TAGs to IEC TC 65 and IEC TC 66. It also holds, through ANSI, the Secretariat for IEC TC 65/SC 65B and ISO TC 10/SC 3.

Until recently, the society has concentrated on creating component-level standards, but it gradually is enlarging its focus to encompass the systems integration level. As this upward move occurs, there will be an opportunity for increasing interaction with the mainstream IT SDOs.

ISA creates standards as an adjunct to its main work, which is to serve as a professional, technical, scientific, and educational society for advancing the state of the art in instrumentation and industrial control. ISA has 41,000 members; 2400 are involved in the standards efforts, serving on 120 standards-writing committees. As of 1988, ISA had published seventy-three standards/recommended practices and currently has sixty draft standards under way.

PART IV. EPILOGUE

15. CURRENT TOPICS
IN STANDARDS

> But Mousie, thou art no thy lane
> In proving foresight may be vain;
> The best-laid schemes o' mice and men
>   Gang aft agley,
> An lea's us not but grief an' pain,
> For promis'd joy!
>
> *To a Mouse*
> Robert Burns

This chapter is a collection of what, in the author's opinion, are high-interest topics in standardization *in the United States* at this time—1989. These are issues of interest and concern in the standards and business community with which we are trying to come to grips in the United States and internationally. Ultimately, action (or not) in these areas will impact the direction and future of standards.

Education and training

This section could be called more appropriately "The *lack of* education and training." Because standards usually has been seen as a technical discipline and because the first U.S. standards organizations were concerned with technical subjects, it might seem reasonable to assume that the technical disciplines are continuing educative efforts in standards. Unfortunately, despite the full curriculum in today's technical schools, there is a distinct paucity of training in this discipline. Engineers are graduating with a great deal of knowledge about how to invent new things but little ability to understand or appreciate the process that creates standards. Granted, the subject is somewhat difficult to teach, since it does not lend itself to quantification, a premier attribute in a technical discipline. Nonetheless, the lack of knowledge of the subject is interesting—some would say appalling—since the body of literature in standards is substantial, representing a cultural heritage that is very impressive and a technical heritage that is very valuable. Yet the average New York City electrician knows more about the practical implementation of building wiring schemes and standards than does the average graduate engineer—because the electrician has been taught to use standards to her/his benefit. The graduate engineer's knowledge of practical application is woefully inadequate and results in unusual, costly, and occasionally defective products.

The lack of training in standards—the process, the concepts, the functionality, the needs—is not solely the responsibility of the technical community, however. The major business schools—and much of academia—seem to regard standards as a nuisance. Because they do not admit of quantification, because they take so long to complete, and because they are difficult to understand and explain, there is a tendency for the process to be ignored in the United States. As a result, a generation of business school graduates is unaware of the U.S. machinery to produce standards and unwilling to attempt to understand the international application of standards. These factors combine to make the entire process substantially more difficult than it need be—especially when resources are needed.

The solution, of course, is to have academic involvement in the standards process. The field needs to be investigated to discover and define how and why the process occurs; it needs to have an idea of why corporations invest; it needs an understanding of its own nature. To learn this, however, active participation is required, which takes time and energy and money. These commodities are in short supply in many instances and, when available, can be devoted to subjects with flashier paybacks. Because it requires hard work and a willingness to learn, this solution will, unfortunately, be unattractive to many academics. And, if there is no understanding, there will be no teaching, except of the type that eventually will have to be unlearned.

The attraction of standards is that they serve to increase commerce in a complex way; they are a fundamental underpinning of society. Yet they are taken for granted; I do not anticipate the establishment of a "Distinguished Lecturer Chair in Standards" at a major institution of higher education. Nonetheless, the area demands study because of its impact: like a glacier, it may only be safely ignored until it begins to move. Standards have begun to move; still, the academicians ignore them.

Organization

One of the more interesting problems that will confront the standards community over the next several years will be where to place the standards function within an organization. It is a problem that will affect providers the most, but users, too, will feel its impact.

If standards are viewed as a marketing tool, then it might seem logical for a provider organization to place them within the marketing function. There is sense to this placement—the marketing department can provide strategic input to the participants to ensure that the organizational goal is achieved, use output from the committees to ensure that the organization is moving in the correct direction, and so forth. But standards are still a technical discipline and, as such, do not respond well to being driven by the marketing function.

Part of the reason for this, I believe, is that marketing in the United States usually takes a somewhat myopic view of problems, emphasizing short-term responses over strategic attempts to keep problems from happening. The old adage about the relative merits of prevention and cure tends to be forgotten. But absolute answers, given with a high degree of assurance, are impractical in the standards arena. Allegiances shift, organizational goals change, and results are not always as planned. If a plan requires a specific response from a standards committee, a very high-risk situation has been set up. The output of a standards committee will be a standard, but the precise nature and shape of the standard is not known until the final vote is cast. Without a strategic plan to keep the outcome of the standards groups in perspective, there is a tendency to change plans with each change in the committee, which results in a surfeit of plans and little actual work.

An additional negative about having the function report to marketing is that marketing and engineering—from whence most of the delegates proceed—are inclined to have a great deal of trouble relating to one another. While they speak a common language, there is a vast gulf between the need that most engineers have for precision and the marketing need for hyperbole. The disciplines work from different philosophical bases, and this can and does cause problems. Sales, a more tactical extension of marketing, is even worse than marketing.

The standards function could report to the financial department, since the basic rationale for standards is economic. Unfortunately, most of the comments that were made about the mismatch of marketing and standards apply equally well to the marriage of standards and the financial group. While the discipline required to manage financial projects might be of use to some standards committees, the lack of a specific return from a standard or committee can be upsetting to most financially oriented people.

Manufacturing, on the other hand, while searching for a standardized method of creating, tends to concentrate on a single, long-term solution, in large part because of the intense capital investment required. This bias is carried over into much of manufacturing's thinking, which emphasizes stability and gradual change. Standards, while usually evolutionary, can be revolutionary at times. And revolution, to an organization that needs smooth flow, can be catastrophic.

Where marketing usually is too focused on the here and now, engineering tends to focus on the challenge of the problem, rather than on its business aspect. Standards, however, are not an end unto themselves—they must serve some business function. Favoring their technical aspects over their business and management aspects overlooks the main reason that standards exist at all.

There are a few other areas where the standards function legitimately could be placed. All of them suffer from organizational foci that usually are not broad enough or strong enough or time sensitive enough to manage the discipline of standards correctly.

The solution to the problem lies not in organizational placement but in the concept of the activity within and without the organization, not in the organization's management but in the management of the standards group. If the standards group sees itself as the champion of one particular discipline, then it will not succeed over the long term. Standards need too much of each discipline—and impact all disciplines too greatly—to refuse the responsibility of cross-disciplinary perception. The management of the standards group must rely on an innate sense of fairness to serve the entire organization, rather than favoring a portion of it.

This puts the burden on the manager of the standards group—and it is not a burden to be taken lightly, since the administration of a standards group is never easy. But the group's placement in the organization is immaterial if its manager understands what the discipline of standards is all about and learns to deal with all of the impacted groups and cultures. If the manager cannot do this, organizational placement is moot.

Resource development

One of the major problems with the increase in standards activities is the scarcity of resources available to standards committees in the United States. These resources are, of course, the participants.

While large numbers of engineers potentially can attend committee meetings, the number who may attend is a good deal smaller. The process that diminishes the potential source of participants is economically driven—as one would expect. To begin, many companies in the United States (and elsewhere, one would suspect) don't really want to be bothered by standards; they are mostly content to accept and implement the standards that are produced. I believe that many providers fall into this group.

At the next level of diminution are the providers who might participate but really cannot afford to have people attend meetings. The cost here is not merely that of travel but also the cost of the person. To be effective in a meeting—that is, to help the committee innovate—the participant must be reasonably competent and skilled in the discipline under consideration. Few providers have a surfeit of this kind of employee. As a result, there is a natural tendency to use the highly competent employee in the more immediate best interests of the organization, rather than in the long-range interests of the industry. The idea seems to be that, when one is fighting a fire, one does not especially care about advances in the architecture of fireproof buildings. Along these same lines, some providers send their most inept employees to meetings, working under the theory that this is where they will do the least harm. And then there are the providers who send representatives only occasionally, which is better than sending no one but is somewhat limiting. It is rather like reading only every third chapter in a book—you have an idea of what is happening but may not be able to follow the plot and draw the right conclusions.

This leaves a relatively small number of viable participants, from which the managers and leaders of the process—the "standards technocrats"—must be drawn. These managerial technocrats are difficult to find, as well as being valuable in other positions in an organization. Usually, in a smaller company, they are the premier line managers. They know how to use technology and people to get things done; at the same time, they are able to deal with complexities and shifting priorities in real time. Add to this the ability to think strategically in an international setting, and the technocrat becomes a precious resource, which normally is of too much utility to the organization to be committed to help the industry by participating in standards. This resource—the standards technocrat/standards manager—is very scarce in the United States. It is less so internationally, where standards are perceived as an essential part of doing business. From this point of view, the United States is at a disadvantage; in regarding standards as a discipline, we lag a little.

From a resource point of view, then, the providers often lack the motivation to participate. Even with the motivation, they often lack commitment to the process, which presupposes a willingness to commit to a long-term effort, using valuable human resources, for a long-term payback. This reluctance reflects American industry's penchant for taking a short term, narrowly centered view of the market, a tendency that—slowly—is changing.

On the other hand, the providers are not the only participants in the process, and the users are equally remiss in their participation. There are several good reasons for this, not the least of which are identical to those that impact the providers. But the lack of user participation stems from an additional series of complications. They tend to believe that they have less power in the committees than do the providers, although the one-vote/one-participant rule puts all delegates on an equal footing. More importantly, very few users can sustain their activity over the length of time that it takes to develop a standard. Users have a shorter time horizon than do providers, and this aspect of the IT industry is more difficult to solve.

The standardization process takes time; users need problems solved. Usually, by the time a problem is visible, there is too little time to solve it with a standard. Providers do try to create standards to solve foreseeable problems, but they cannot solve those of obscure origin—that is, those problems unique to application disciplines about which little is known except by the users. The standards consortia are a response to this problem—one that I feel will not succeed as well as would sufficient commitment to the extant process.

In the end, then, the resource problem is a commitment problem. Resources are available, but only if there is a commitment to the process that needs the resources. If organizations believe that the process can and will work for them, then resources will be made available. As of 1989, the United States appears ambivalent; standards are in, but the commitment—and hence the necessary resources—

isn't. Until this attitude changes, there will be continuing problems with adequate coverage of all standards activities in the United States, and this, in turn, will impact much of the rest of the world.

The process

The standards process, in its present form, is a curious combination of naiveté and sophistication. The process depends on the goodwill of a large population for the successful creation of standards and on enlightened self-interest for the successful completion of the process (that is, the use of the standards produced). Both of these attributes are potentially unreliable and, in terms of human behavior, entirely unnatural. However, the process works and seems to work well. But for how much longer?

The genius of the consensus process is that it is based on the free cooperation and willing participation of all of the parties involved. No force compels the use of consensus standards; rather, their creation and use represents a collective willingness to believe that the market (or whatever one believes to be the force that selects the successful activities) can and will continue to operate without impediment—or with only minimal impediment. This faith is being tested but probably will survive the trial.

A secondary corollary of the process is that all who wish to participate can, and all can see the results of their work. This rapidly is becoming a critical area. Standards no longer can be developed in isolation, and the responsibility to take into account the interests and needs of all directly and materially impacted parties puts a tremendous strain on the consensus process. Curiously, the strain is due to the success with which the process attracts converts. With the move away from proprietary solutions in the area of IT, increasing numbers of participants and interests are joining the consensus process. And, as the number of participants increases, so does the number of potential interactions. With the increase in the number of interactions comes a concomitant increase in the time needed to complete the interactions, and standards creation gradually slows down. This intensifies the need for standards, causing more standards to be started to complement those under development and placing even greater demands on an already overloaded system. It also dilutes the resources for any single standards effort, since there are more projects initiated than there are human resources committed.

One possible response is to match the input to the output, following the principle behind the parental dictum, "You can't have any more until you've finished what is on your plate." This approach sounds reasonably simple to implement, and the idea would be excellent if all standards were relatively equal to one another and the consensus standards process were their only source. But alternatives do exist, and all standards are not equal. Moreover, the need for standardization continues to grow. Only a few standards would be required in a Walden Pond utopia; in today's environment, Thoreau's cry to simplify is not only ignored but unheard.

Limiting standards to those that are needed begs the problem. The parental decree becomes "You can only have what is good for you." The question that springs to mind is, good by whose definition? *De gustibus non est disputandum* (There is no disputing about tastes) applies here: my definition of what is needed may disagree with another's; it is impossible to draw moral distinctions and define "good" and "bad" absolutely. Rather, the consensus process—or the market— will agree on a definition. To do so, however, all cases and causes must be considered.

The solution does not lie in the mechanics of the standards process. Expediting the handling of paper would have little effect since the same deliberations between the same number of people still would have to take place. The process requires that people take time to think about and digest the implications of a standard; in a systems environment, there is much to consider before reaching an opinion. Anticipatory systems standards—such as OSI—require extensive advance conceptualization before development can begin. Chapter 5 noted that three stages must occur before a standard can be written. These stages only now are coming into prominence, yet it is in these stages—preconceptualization, conceptualization, and discussion—that the process can be improved and made stronger; the writing of the standard, while easier and more amenable to automation, is just the more-or-less mechanical distillation of the work that has gone on before.

The purpose of standardization is not paper; it is the production of a meaningful set of shared concepts and beliefs on a certain subject. Once this shared set of understandings is established, the time required to produce the standard can be reduced. As noted, however, the first stages require planning and thought. Also as noted, the people who can do this thinking are fairly rare. And with no emphasis on training new standards professionals, their population is not increasing. This, more than any other defect in the standards discipline, poses a threat to the process.

16. IN DEFENSE

OF HETEROGENEITY

> Were I so tall to reach the pole
> Or grasp the ocean with my span,
> I must be measured by my soul,
> The mind's the standard of the man.
>
> *True Greatness*
> Isaac Watts

When I began this book nearly three years ago, I was searching for a single underlying principle to describe the standards discipline that would establish it as a science, rather than an art. I was looking for a quantifiable or qualifiable characteristic or set of characteristics that would define the world of standardization—that would make explication easy.

I have found that principle, and I think that it shows most clearly in the definition of standards and standardization in Chapter 3. The key to the discipline—or the genius of the process—rests with the participants and the immense diversity that they bring to the arena. The survival of the consensus process does not lie in the definition of the standards discipline but in the participants' understanding that diversity and the acceptance and use of this diversity are what enables the process.

The transition of a concept from a vague idea to a product takes time and, more importantly, planning. Planning, then, becomes the crucial attribute of the standards process. Without planning, the process probably will not work, since all of the effort will be wasted on here-and-now topics that disappear with time. With completely centralized planning, too, there is no chance for the process to work, since it depends on diversity to craft a position that has examined nearly all of the potentialities from nearly every position. The strength of the process, then, derives from the participants in the process—but in a rather unusual fashion. It is not a function of the number of participants or the degree of participation or the degree of wisdom; rather, it grows from the ability of the participants to understand what they are trying to accomplish—to provide the IT industry with a reasoned and executable path into the future.

Ultimately, the process is an education for all concerned. The delegates must know when to hold on to a principle and when to give up on principles that are held for convenience. The organizations that support the delegates—from single-person companies to the largest multinationals—must know or learn when to fight and when to withdraw. Certain principles cannot or should not be compromised, but, all too often, a position is defended because it is easier to be dogmatic than to understand what is really going on.

The heterogeneous nature of the committees is also the essential weakness of this approach to standards, since achieving consensus takes time and patience. The antidote is to understand what the committees are trying to achieve. The anticipatory systems standard—in which a systems concept is submitted for standardization prior to implementation in the industry—is one of the more difficult tasks a consensus committee can undertake, but it is uniquely suited to the strengths and forgiving of the weaknesses of the consensus process. It is a concept that the consensus committees of the IT community are pioneering.

Standards and standardization are change agents—change agents that depend on the abilities of the participants for survival. A standard's very nature requires the heterogeneous makeup of the committees; if a solution represents a true consensus, it becomes a synergistic plan that will carry the industry into a new and different arena. And without this structured change, the industry will not continue to grow. Robert Browning once noted:

Ah, that a man's reach should exceed his grasp
Or what's a heaven for?

The standardization process and standards help the industry to keep moving, to keep wanting, to keep achieving, to keep changing. This, more than anything else, is the ultimate rationale for standards.

INDEX

American National Standards
Institute (ANSI) (*cont.*)
formation of, 159–160
future of, 163–164, 168
government and, 160
HFS and, 218
international standards and, 163
ISA and, 220
ISO and, 132, 133
membership in, 163, 164
organization of, 164–168
problems of, 162–164
procedures of, 168–170
sales of standards by, 168
technological change and, 162, 168
telecommunications industry and,
181
American Society for Testing and
Materials (ASTM), 21
American Society of Mechanical En-
gineers, 21
American Telephone and Telegraph,
180
ANSI. *See* American National Stan-
dards Institute (ANSI)
Appeals Board, ANSI, 167
Application Portability Working
Group, JTC 1, 135
Architecture, 70
Articles of Convention, ITU, 143
ASC T1, 180–186
membership in, 182
organization of, 182–186
procedures of, 186
purpose of, 180–182
ASC T1 Advisory Group (T1AG),
184–186
ASC X12, 217–218
ASC X3. *See* X3
ASC X3T9.5, 31
ASC Z39, 219–220
Associate members, ECMA, 152–154

Association Française de Normalisation (AFNOR), 192–195
membership in, 193
organization of, 193–194
procedures of, 194–195
purpose of, 192–193
ASTM. *See* American Society for
Testing and Materials (ASTM)

Board of Directors, ANSI, 164
Board of Standards Review, ANSI,
167, 169–170, 202–204
British Standards Institute (BSI),
158, 198
Brooks Act (1965), 212–213, 214
Browning, Robert, 234–235
Business schools, 224
Byzantine Roman Empire, 14

Canadian Electrical Codes, 189
Canadian Standards Association
(CSA), 186–189
membership in, 187
organization of, 187–188
procedures, 188–189
purpose of, 186–187
Canvass method. *See* Accredited
Sponsor standardization method
Capitalism, 15
Carnegie-Mellon University, 8
CASCO, 167
CBEMA. *See* Computer and Busi-
ness Equipment Manufacturers
Association (CBEMA)
CCIR, 143
CCITT. *See* International Telegraph
and Telephone Consultive Coop-
erative
Central Secretariat (ISO), 129–130
Certification, CEN, 156
Certification and Testing Group,
CSA, 187

Consensus standards (*cont.*)
for reinforcing industry patterns, 29
standards organizations and, 91
technological change and, 118–120, 118–121
user/provider issues, 27–28, 39–41
Consensus standards process, 103–112, 230–232
Accredited Organization method of, 105–106
Accredited Sponsor method of, 103–104
Accredited Standards Committee method of, 106–108
checks-and-balances system in, 105, 108–110
common good and, 109
costs of, 108
effectiveness of, 112
expectations for, 110–111
expertise required for, 105
interest groups and, 105
methods of, 103–108
openness of, 109
role of professionals in, 116–117
technical implementation and, 109
time required for, 110–111
Consumer Interest Council, ANSI, 166
Control, 97
Conveners, ISO, 130
Coordinating Committee, ECMA, 153
Coordination, 98
Corporate Affairs, CSA, 187
Corporation for Open Systems (COS), 208, 209–210
Correspondent member, ISO, 127
Council, ISO, 127, 129
Country organizations, 93–94
Craft guilds, 15

CSA. *See* Canadian Standards Association (CSA)
CSA Information Update, 189
Cultural standards, 13

Deutsches Institut für Normung e.V. (DIN), 189–192
membership in, 191–192
organization of, 191–192
procedures of, 192
purpose of, 189–191
Digital Equipment Corporation, 63
Discussion, 69, 72–74, 232
Draft International Standard (DIS), ISO, 131
Draft Proposal (DP), ISO, 131
Draft proposed American National Standards (dpANS), 169–170, 175
Duplicability, 16

ECMA. *See* European Computer Manufacturers Association (ECMA)
ECSA, 181, 184
Economic power, of standards bodies, 95
Economics, of standards, 4–5, 7–8, 10–11
Education and training, lack of, 223–225
Electrical engineering standards, 126
Electricity standards, 138–139
Electronic data interchange (EDI), 217–218
Electronic engineering standards, 126
Electronics Industries Association (EIA), 206–208
Electrotechnical standards, 138–139

Standards Steering Committees
(SSCs), CSA, 188
State Department, U.S., 143, 182,
210–212
Stater, 13–14
State regulation, 16–17, 19
Strategic planning. *See* Planning
Strategic Planning Working Group,
JTC 1, 135
Study groups (SGs), CCITT, 146
Subcommittees (SCs), ISO, 130, 131
SWGs, 135
Systems profile, 49–50, 52
System standardization, 36

Tarbell, Ida, 17
Taylor, Frederick, 21
TC X3J4 (COBOL), 177
Technical Activities Board, IEEE,
202
Technical Board, ISO, 129
Technical committees (TCs), 117
ASC T1, 184–186
CSA, 188
ECMA, 152–154
IEC, 139, 141
ISO, 126, 130
X3, 175–177
Technical engineering/business man-
agers, 88
Technical implementation, 109
Technical Office Protocol (TOP),
208, 209
Technological change
consensus standards and, 118–120
standards bodies and, 200
Telecommunications industry, 126
ASC T1 and, 180–182
CCITT and, 146
efficiency of, 142–143
standards for, 36, 214
Transportation Data Coordinating
Committee, 217

Turf wars, 94

United Kingdom, BSI and, 198
United Nations, 142
United States
ANSI and, 160
current standards topics in, 223–
232
United States Organization for the
International Telegraph and
Telephone Consultative Committee (U.S. CCITT), 211–
212
ASC T1 and, 182
User groups, 199–201. *See also*
Professional associations
EIA, 206–210
IEEE, 201–206
problems with, 118, 200–201
role of, 120
standardized specifications written
by, 50
Users
awareness of standards by, 75
bias toward, 54
consensus standards and, 115
external standardization and, 70–
71
forecasting needs of, 115–116
functional profiles and, 50
interest in standards by, 68
vs. providers, 27–28, 39–41, 47–
48, 50
standards committee participation
by, 47
standards group interdependency
and, 117
standards needs of, 54–56
systems profiles for, 49–50
U.S. Joint Technical Committee 1
Technical Advisory Group (U.S.
JTC 1 TAG), 178–180